Lives; Running

Lives; Running

David Renton

Winchester, UK
Washington, USA

First published by Zero Books, 2012
Zero Books is an imprint of John Hunt Publishing Ltd., Laurel House, Station Approach,
Alresford, Hants, SO24 9JH, UK
office1@o-books.net
www.o-books.com

For distributor details and how to order please visit the 'Ordering' section on our website.

ISBN: 978 1 78099 235 8

A CIP catalogue record for this book is available from the British Library.

Design: Stuart Davies

Printed in the USA by Edwards Brothers Malloy

CONTENTS

6 x 200 metres 1

The Rivals 5

Learning To Run 11

The Red Vest 25

Injured 32

A Real Racer Who Never Tires 36

1.59.7 48

My Father's Diary 54

The Grimace 58

Defeat 64

Love, Spiritual Or Otherwise 72

After Rivalry 76

Triumph 82

Conversion 86

Learning to Run Again 90

Boys 104

Now 108

6 x 200 metres

I have a short, stilted, stride. I do not stretch, rather I scuttle like a clubfooted beetle. For most of my running life, I have pounded my lower legs, relying on my calves to generate speed. My tread is heavy, my feet push against the ground. The force carries them back, up behind my knees. Years ago I ran a cross-country race. Afterwards, the back of my vest was covered with sploshes of muddy water: kicked back and up by my feet. I looked at the other competitors. They were lighter as they ran. They were proper long-distance runners, their tops, unlike mine, were clean.

My weight lands more on my toes than my heel. When I turn over my running shoes the top half of each is worn down. From left to right, the rubber protecting my toes is just a few millimetres thick. The heel shows no signs of wear.

At my fastest my arms forced me round the track. I held them tight, a boxer punching an opponent in the ribs. I faced the track front on, my back straight. I used my upper body to push my legs forwards. I neither ran nor jogged; I raced.

Running was part of my life, I ran whenever I could. Twelve years old, walking home through London, I saw two older boys approach and sensed what felt like steps towards a fight. Refusing to pause, unwilling to admit that the situation might be less threatening than I had guessed, I sprinted off, leaving them behind.

In the villages near where my aunt lived there were a group of children, every age from five to thirteen. I challenged the two cyclists in the group to race after race along narrow country lanes. We raced, I sprinted; I was always first.

Skipping school, a year later, a friend and I caught the eye of two police officers in a marked car. I had thrown a coke bottle towards a bin and missed. The glass broke loud on the ground. The officers, watching, brought their car to a halt. "Meet at the park", I shouted. My words must have magnified the officers' suspicions. My friend went in one direction; I went the other, running against the flow of one-way streets. Thirty minutes later, we met again, the police nowhere to be seen. My friend's chest heaved to fill his lungs with air.

My racing peak came three years later: I was training at my school athletics track; the surface had just been freshly laid. Red tartan, replacing black cinders, my feet bounced high on it like a triple jumper's as I ran. I was in a pack of five or six boys; I was the fastest among them. We ran a training session of 200 metre intervals, six lots of 200 metre sprints followed by 200 metres of jog recovery. We were timed by hand. Each 200 metre sprint I ran in under 25 seconds. Afterwards, I jogged the mile back to my room. The effort of the sprints left no greater trace than a thin layer of salt on my face. The very next day I ran a further six by 200 metres session at the same speed.

I was always on the verge of sprinting. I could run at almost maximum pace for longer than any other runner I knew.

Now, when I run just a mile, I am left with stiffness in my back, pain in my groin, in the ligaments of my foot and in my right knee, tightness in my left achilles tendon. My recovery takes days.

In a picture in my bedroom there are fifteen members of the school athletics team, six of us sit in front on chairs while a further nine, mostly field athletes, stand with their arms crossed behind. There are two other middle distance runners in the front row: Peter who ran for England as a student, Tom who was later an international triathlete. I raced Tom many, many times. We trained together; we raced against our counterparts in other school teams. He was not a faster runner than me.

Before us and on every side, the track is a deep red. One or two wisps of dead grass have blown onto the track but otherwise its surface is pristine. It looks wonderfully well-kept; it is unlike any other track on which I ran.

I stare at my photograph in bewilderment; my hair was so long, my face so thin. I can barely recall the person who sits in my place. I had beaten the school records for 800 metres at the ages of 14 and 16. Alone in the picture, I do not look straight into the camera. It was one of the last times I was content in that team.

I never rowed. I loved watching cricket, and played a little but hated the feel of the hard leather ball stinging my hands, arms, or legs. I played football often enough but my first touch was leaden and I had no natural sense of the other players' positions on the field. I chose a position, right full back, where my involvement narrowed down to one-on-one confrontations. The other team's full back would run at me with the ball. A few minutes later, our situations reversed, I would race back at him.

I did not do weights, I was not encouraged to mix my track sessions with swimming, cycling or yoga. It does not seem to have occurred to any of my coaches that running was a repetitive exercise. To train for an 800m race, I ran. Variation involved the exchange only of short distance sprints for longer runs at ideally a gentler speed. The more effort I would put in to my running, the more I strained the same parts of my body and the more likely I made it that my legs would give way.

Today, I feel the legacy of my former training. I was running myself lame.

I have raced along summer beaches and across frozen lakes. I have sprinted along canals and beside riverbanks. Once, I raced a friend around two laps of the largest outdoor swimming pool in Europe, the bathers lifting their legs upwards in an attempt to catch our trailing feet. I ran on the day of the worst storms the country had ever known, battling the wind on the way out, my fingers pointing out and up, my head ten degrees forwards of vertical. On the way back, I ran the same four miles even faster, jubilant at my speed, triumphing over nature. There were many victories.

I have run in joy, I have run in so many kinds of pain. I have pulled each of my tendons, torn the small muscles in my knee, turned the insides of my lungs brown with infection, known my upper legs in agony. I have improvised many painkillers: oranges, water, sports drinks and on one occasion sweets.

Today, the din of my feet on gravel is ponderously slow; my loud lumping pace scares the animals on the ground and the birds in the trees. I run slowly and without style, just like a dad dancing.

The Rivals

For my parents, the 1966 World Cup was the moment when black and white television was replaced by colour. For me, the 1980 Olympics was the point at which a hand-tuned TV set finally gave way to pre-set channels and a remote control. I was seven years old and fed up of watching Grange Hill on the upstairs set, a black and white set with a 16-inch screen that required retuning at 45 second intervals. I knew from my father that Seb Coe and Steve Ovett would dominate the 800 and 1500 metres and for the first time since I was very young I would be allowed to watch the finals on my parents' room-sized colour Sony downstairs.

The news had been building up to the Olympics over the previous seven months. Multiple British victories were, as ever, confidently expected. Yet the mood of the coverage was far from upbeat.

In April, dragged into line by President Carter, the US Olympic Committee had voted to boycott the Moscow Olympics. For several weeks afterwards, it seemed possible that the British Olympic Association might follow their lead. Our Prime Minister wrote to all British athletes urging them to boycott the games too.

Others joined the American effort: loyal Israel, Kenya, Morocco, West Germany, Canada and even Red China. Where there is discord, the Prime Minister had said, may we bring harmony. But these were the last days of amateur athletics, our competitors were pressing hard against the limits of the convention that they should not be paid, and success at the Olympics was the way to get invited to the better-remunerated European events. By a large majority, the British Olympic Association voted to leave the choice to individual athletes. The athletes in turn voted to compete, and who would blame them?

The sprinter Alan Wells ran the 100 metres in the white of Great Britain rather than his usual Scottish blue. Would he have won gold had the Americans been there? He would not have won had the Cuban athlete who came second merely better timed his dip for the line.

Even in the press there were voices calling for British participation. Three weeks before the Olympic finals, Ovett was in Oslo where he broke the world record for the mile. The *Express* dubbed his and Coe's performances a "tonic" which could not "be bad for a country suffering the economic blues".

My father allowed me to watch the 800 metre final, the showdown between Coe and Ovett. Coe was the media's champion and my father's clear favourite. He was lithe, where Ovett was muscular. He had the veneer of a public school boy. His coach and father Peter was a manager and former amateur cyclist who had dedicated his own life to developing his son's athletic career.

In the 800 metres, Coe ran greyhound-swift, he was happiest in the very fastest of races. Pulled through the first lap by a pacesetter, the field would thin out, leaving him in the perfect position to sprint for a record. The summer before the Olympics, his world records over 800, 1500 metres and the mile had all been shown live on TV.

Ovett's family were market traders, they saw athletics as just another business. Their son flourished amid the heat of competition. His home distance was 1500 metres. Biding his time to the last 150 metres, he would remain on the shoulder of the race leader. Poised to strike, he would kick for the line. Whether the race was slow or fast, he seemed able to pull out this finish whenever it was needed.

As we waited for the 800 metre heats and then the final,

highlights of past races were replayed including Coe and Ovett's five world records over the past 12 months, Ovett's triumph at the World Cup in 1977, and Coe's victory at the European Cup in 1979. Yet alongside these victories, other footage was also shown.

One clip showed Ovett's defeat at the 1976 Olympics in Montreal. Placed in the eighth lane, he had struggled as a result of the authorities' decision to run the first 300 metres of the race in lanes. He did not want to go out too fast for fear of diminishing his best weapon, his finishing kick. In the fifth lane was Alberto Juantorena, 6'2" and 185lbs of 400 metre sprinter experimenting with a distance at which he had barely previously raced. After 300 metres, Ovett was well down on Juantorena. Out in lane eight, he had no idea of the gap. The sprinter reeled off laps of 51 and 52 seconds, not merely winning but breaking the world record. Ovett finished fifth.

"I dedicate this gold medal to Fidel Castro and the revolution", Juantorena told the press afterwards, the journalists smirking at his commitment.

Coe's moment came a year later, when he broke the UK 800 metres record coming second at Crystal Palace to Kenya's Mike Boit. Coe and Ovett then clashed over 800 metres at the 1978 European championships in Prague. It was the first meeting between the two runners since they had been schoolboys.

The race began with Coe, the younger athlete and still in awe of Ovett, seeking to recreate Juantorena's dash at Montreal. He ran the first lap of the Prague 800 metres in 49.3 seconds. Had he been capable of running the second lap at the same pace he would have broken the world record by five seconds. But, of course, he tired. With 300 metres to go Ovett eased past Olaf Beyer in third, and made his way to Coe's shoulder. "Beyer is finished", the commentator said. Ovett then passed Coe 150 metres from the line. I was astonished at how relaxed Ovett seemed. But he could not pull away; instead Beyer came back into the race and caught Ovett at the line.

Ovett jogged to a halt, looked for his parents in the crowd, smiled, and shrugged. He comforted Coe as they walked together from the track.

My father told me that Coe was the better runner. Loyal, I followed him in rooting for Coe. But through the 800 metre heats I saw something which shook my resolve. It was not that Coe ran badly, his winning time in the first 800 metre heat (1.48.5) was a second faster than Ovett's. Coe seemed to me to run lightly on the track and with grace. His legs did not tire; he wasted no energy as he ran.

At the end of the race I saw Ovett, his face broken into a smile, looking for the camera as the camera searched for him. He looked deeply into it, and I saw him mouth the words "I love you". If there was any doubt, he traced the letters "ILY" with the fingers of his left hand as he spoke. The recipient of the message, although I could not know this at the time, since even the commentators were confused and trying to make sense of the words, was his girlfriend left behind in England.

I grasped only this, that Ovett saw sport as pleasure, as a second priority in his life. Ovett overtook Coe as my hero at that moment.

I knew that Ovett was seen as arrogant. To my father's mind, it was a simple matter of heredity. Ovett meant to break apart the amateur cabal and promised to do so in the name of the self-employed worker. Amateurism my father considered indefensible, it would in time have to be pulled apart (as a businessman he saw the whole issue as a simple restraint of trade). Ovett was however the wrong person to carry out the task. Go, amateurism must, but on Coe's and not on Ovett's terms.

Ovett was undoubtedly the villain of the piece. The papers said so, the commentators on television alluded to some vague and unspecified flaws in his character. But what his real crimes were, no-one seemed to be able to say. It was suggested at times that he was unpatriotic, hinted that he had been given opportunities to run for Great Britain and had turned them down. But from the crowd, I seemed to hear an extra enthusiasm when he ran. You could hear the crowd, even in Moscow, shouting "O-vett, O-vett". I could hear no similar chants for Coe.

Ovett's face was still, his eyes cool. He made winning look so easy.

"The two Britons have all the options", the commentator David Coleman told his viewers, "so long as they don't become hypnotised with the obsession of beating each other." Coe was in a blue sweatshirt to warm up; his jaw was wobbling with the anxiety of it all.

There was no Juantorena this time. Coe too was determined not to repeat his mistake of 1978 and made his way into the race only slowly from the back. Ovett spent the first 300 metres being jostled in sixth and seventh. With 420 metres to go, he ran up to the two East Germans in front of him, and attempted to prise them apart, his arms parting them like a swimmer doing the breast-stroke. Ovett made his way into fourth, the runners in front leaving space on their inside as they failed to overtake on the outside other competitors ahead of them. Coe was still in eighth, running wide into the third lane. Eighty metres from the line, Ovett made his way to the front. Coe's late sprint took him to within five metres of his rival but no closer.

Ovett looked to his parents and waved both his fists in their direction.

Coe had to make do with the burden of his father and coach, Peter, who made a point of chastising him publicly on his defeat. "You ran like an idiot," Peter Coe told him. Peter then kept up a commentary of insults which continued until the press conference afterwards. "You ran like a cunt", Peter told his son, the journalists listening. The British press mourned Ovett's victory; the common sentiment was that the "Bad Guy" had won. At the awards ceremony, when Ovett turned to him and held out his hand, Coe's eyes, already focussed far beyond Ovett's shoulder, did not move. Coe accepted his silver medal gracelessly. There were rumours that he was now considering quitting the sport altogether.

The sole hope for the younger runner was in the heats of the 1500 metres, due to start in just four days' time. It would be the same format, two heats and a final. "Get your finger out Coe, I've got money on you," read a cable from home.

But Coe had just come second at his favourite distance. Ovett had won 45 consecutive races at 1500 metres or the mile since he had last been beaten, three years before.

The first lap of the 1500 metres was run in 61.6 seconds. If that was slow, the second lap, at 63.3 seconds, was slower still. Six hundred metres from home an East German athlete Jürgen Straub determined to make a race of it. He ran the next 600 metres in bursts of 26 seconds, a speed that would have come close to winning the 800 metres final. At the bell, Coe was three metres behind Straub, and Ovett a further two metres behind. I was certain that Ovett would win. In the final straight, Ovett pulled wide to Coe's outside, and his stride lengthened, but without making up any ground.

By the time Coe caught up with Straub, 120 metres from the line, Ovett was so close that he could almost touch his rival. It would surely be a moment's work for him to pass. With 90 metres to go, Coe had increased his lead over Ovett to a further metre, but still Ovett's victory seemed certain. He was sprinting now, and yet the gap did not narrow. Coe duly won, Ovett finishing eight metres behind in third.

Coe's face, as he crossed the line, was like a death mask.

Learning To Run

It is a spring day. I am with my parents, at my grandparents' home. It is a wooden cottage, with a back lawn and stone paths. The sun is high above and I know it will be lunchtime soon. Before, my parents used to have a country house of their own, with trees to climb and a well. They have sold that home to spend their weekends with my grandparents (my grandfather will die just a year later). My mother and I have been admiring flowers in the garden. One day my parents will live there. In the future, I am told, the house will be mine. Look at the flowers, my mother says, they will be yours. On the path back to the house, I want my father to race me. I already know that my father is older than the other parents at school.

I charge off ahead. I am running for the pleasure of speed in my legs, to be free in movement, for the joy of being alive. I run also to escape the attention of my grandparents in whose company I feel awkward.

My father does not join me in running but merely walks behind.

I was a slender, cautious child. I enjoyed lessons and was enthusiastic when the teachers asked me questions. I took pleasure in learning something new. I read and re-read every book in our school library. I wrote.

I made friendships, but kept them going only with difficulty. I avoided the choir, drama, refused to learn a musical instrument, and ignored all the other modest activities that were intended to bring children together outside the classroom. I did not enjoy playing football and disliked the company of the boys who were best at it. My closest friends I made among the children who dreamed. One was an artist, who painted dragons and knights in armour; my drawings by contrast were stick figures. Another was a poet, who understood with me that there was a world of politics outside the classroom. A third friend invented one week a new school currency, made of pieces of tin foil that the other children belatedly agreed to trade with him, draining into their hands his whole week's pocket money.

I was lonely. All children endure long periods during which they are profoundly unhappy. I relied on my parents to navigate a way through for me.

My journey towards running was made easier by the one exercise which I and my parents shared. At Christmas and at Easter (my father's work allowing), my parents would take me skiing for a week, to Switzerland, Austria or Italy. I recall these holidays with pleasure, for the subtle, bitter tang of apple juice in German-speaking Switzerland, for the sachets of Nutella with breakfast in Italian hotels.

In the mornings I would ski with the local ski school, in the afternoon I joined up with my parents. I loathed the ski schools with abandon. I detested the children who skied better than me, I even despised those who were my equals. I found it hard to make friends. I do not recall ever meeting the same classmate twice.

My mother had learned to ski before she left school and skied without difficulty. She kept her skis close together, turning her hips gracefully from side to side. My father's skiing by contrast was hard-won. He had learned the sport late. He would end his meals early, forcing himself to practice, to make himself learn. Almost all of his frustration as a late adopter he kindly restrained when trying to teach me.

The part of my skiing which pained my father most was my inability to improve. I disliked in particular the weight of my skis, the pain in my shoulders when I carried them for any distance. I groaned at the repetitiveness of the exercise: at the so many times I was made to walk sideways up a slope, the heaviness of my boots and skis as I raised my legs and readied my body to turn. I was too light to descend with any speed and I lacked the momentum at which the sport becomes enjoyable. I remained too long at the same point, uninterested in off-piste, equally ungainly as I descended, no more brave. My father would take me to the top of steep hills, promising fields of snow, covering me to the height of my chest. I wanted only to be allowed fast valleys instead.

I attempted all the tricks of a child, mislaying my skis, sticks, or gloves. I was trying to break up the routine of the exercise, impose myself on the sport.

My father retaliated with infinite patience, finding whatever it was I had dropped. He walked with me, encouraged me, and sometimes I learned.

Skiing fast downhill places pressure on a skier's legs. Feet grip the slope. The skier has to hold their knees together. Absorbing the force works lungs and heart. I acquired something I had not acknowledged before, a taste for speed. Skiing made parts of me strong, the same parts that later enabled me to run.

Less happily, when I was aged five, we spent a week skiing in North Italy. That year, the weather was unusually cold, with temperatures as low as minus twenty five. The wind scraped our faces, as we queued to ascend by gondola. I was wearing a red padded ski-suit, with several layers of clothes beneath, a woollen hat and scarf. Through all these layers, I still felt the cold in my flesh and in my bones.

I disliked this ski school more than most. My fellow pupils were mostly French; I could no more speak to them than they to me. If there were other children who spoke some English, I had no success in finding them. The instructors complained that I skied too fast and without control. I was seen as reckless; I was treated as a beginner and demoted into a beginner's class.

A day or so afterwards, the worst of the cold had eased a little, I found myself in the middle of a ski-school crocodile, ten children following each other in a line. The ground was flat. I turned towards my left, allowing my weight to swing in, towards the slope. As I turned the lower edge of my top ski caught on a patch of grey ice, I slid and fell. So far, the fall was nothing unusual. It was only as I attempted to stand that I realised my leg could not take my weight. My left side, on which I still felt no pain, buckled. It was like trying to walk with one foot on land and the other in water.

The instructor, seeing me confused and unable to stand, skied, with me holding on to his back, fast down the hill. In due course a doctor explained that when I had fallen I had broken both the bones of my left leg. The breaks were just above the ankle, where the weight of my body had taken my leg across the top of my boots.

It is the same calf muscle which I have injured repeatedly since.

Around my sixth birthday, I was in the kitchen with my mother. I recall the low blue table at which I ate; beside it was an orange wooden box which had once held twelve bottles of tonic water. Our dog was somewhere near my feet. I suppose that I must have asked what the things were on the shelves far above my head. "Your father's cups", my mother answered. "When he was young, he was a rower."

The trophies remain frustratingly vague in my memory. I have a sense of tarnished silver, but no memory of their size or shape.

Rowing, I did understand, after a fashion. My parents kept a yacht on the South coast. Sailing was my father's favourite weekend pastime. We would moor sometimes in a dock, sometimes out at sea. Often, the harbour, where most nights we ate, was a boat ride away. My father would set about inflating our dinghy from a foot pump, testing it to be sure that the rubber was absolutely tight, then lowering it into the water. He would then row us to the shore, his great forearms moving with precision. My mother and I would wait as the ground neared.

The yacht was kept for six months on dry land, being prepared for the sailing season. My father would check the outdoor motor, and search the boat for cracks into which water might leak. He would re-paint her hull, her keel. Layers of red and white paint were added by hand. The boat is immaculate in my memory. My parents' friends were invited to help out. I tried to keep them company, waiting till they tired, when I would follow them to the shop to buy cigarettes.

"There were rowers he beat", a friend of my father told me, "who rowed in the Olympics".

Beyond the boat was a slope, after that a wood. I recall other children my age, their hands helping me into a tree. Once, three of us sat proud on top, mastering the view on every side. I remember paths worn by feet, routes between brambles and nettles. I chased other boys my age and was chased back by them in turn, sprinting away from them. I recall also the initial panic among my friends at the presence of girls, the gradual composure of the older boys, their unspoken determination that they should be in control.

Summers, I spent often with my aunt. My father was keen to take the boat sailing for weeks on end. I disliked the corrupted, sweet smell of unburned diesel; it rested in my stomach and made me feel unwell. I disliked also the angle of the boat as it keeled to turn, leaving those sat on its deck facing downwards on a sharp angle towards the sea. While my conscious brain knew that we would of course not drown, I felt ill at ease, and often said so, reducing my parents' own pleasure in the sport.

We reached a compromise under which I would travel for a week each summer to Stratford upon Avon, sharing my aunt's circle of artists and actors, social drinkers, self-employed painters and photographers. My favourite place to run in Stratford was Shottery Fields, a square mile of municipal land, cut by a centuries-old ditch and furrow. There were football pitches on the fields. I would run short laps around the pitches followed by a dozen or more long laps of the park. I tried to run on grass whenever I could.

As a child, twenty years before, Seb Coe had run on the same fields.

I was also running at home, my shortest route took me once around our nearest park, which was about half a mile. When I felt more adventurous, I would run laps of a second nearby park, past football pitches, tennis courts and even a physic garden, home to wood pigeons, mice and frogs, pike from the Canary islands, bushes of thyme and rosemary and statutes of the people who had built the streets all around.

Running was one of a wider set of pleasures, along with watching TV or playing on my computer, seeing friends, listening to bands of my choice and reading to myself. There had been a time when I went nowhere without my parents. I was already reaching an age when I was old enough to choose to be alone.

I ran to be out of the house, on my own with my thoughts. I ran in the spring and summer. I ran in the weeks and not at weekends. I had no formed plans to turn my running into a competitive sport. I ran because I enjoyed the feeling of my body when it was utterly relaxed. I ran for pleasure, I ran because I could.

A kindly absence for most of the evening, my father left work early and partied late. He would return to our house and bathe before friends came round. Our family would be assembled at all points of the dining room table, my father at the head, my mother and I to each side, the dog near the back of the room hoping for scraps. We were gathered to provide an audience for my father's stories; we were the backdrop against which he shone. He could be very funny.

He retired early, in his early fifties. He had no office, just the basement of our house, which he slowly took over with so many files and pieces of loose paper that no free inch of carpet or table was left. My father had plans to launch businesses, a scheme to found an investment trust. He was interviewed in the financial press. His products were on sale in newspaper supplements.

My father bought trainers and began to run, they seemed impossibly large to me on the floor. For him, running was an acknowledgment of middle age. He jogged, running along the main road, the air wobbling with the fumes of passing cars.

On occasion, my father and I ran together. He realised that this was the one sport in which I showed any promise. In his kindness, he wanted to encourage me to develop. Perhaps, he just enjoyed running with another person. I was bought jogging shoes, a big step up from my previous plimsolls. Together, we ran out, at a slow, pedantic pace. We crossed one road, then another. Our pace remained the same. We were too slow; the exercise gave me little pleasure. I wanted to explore the limits of my speed. I saw no joy in testing my body by just running further than before.

If we had to run, my view was that we should talk. My father disagreed; we were in the middle of the city. Talking filled our lungs still further with car fumes. But if we were trying to avoid pollution, why were we running on the busiest main roads?

We ran only once or twice together. After that, the experiment continued no further. I admit that I was the one who ended it. How much better it would have been if we had continued to jog together, even for just a few weeks more.

The fastest pupil at my prep school was a blond ten-year-old boy,

Jimmy. The school's buildings constituted the four corners of a rectangle, and our teacher, struggling to break the habit of our football competitions, timed us racing each other along this route. Jimmy came first. A month later, the race was re-run, save that we were staggered leaving, with Jimmy the last to go. Again, he won, but this time there was a competitive finish, with Jimmy only just catching a group of us at the line.

For the third race, I determined to split the rectangle in the middle, running half a circuit, to finish before Jimmy could catch me. I won but my time was implausibly fast. I confessed quickly and was not punished for cheating.

I was an awkward-to-place December birth, too young for my year, too old for the year below. Following discussions between my teachers and my parents, I dropped down a year. This was a prize, odd as it sounds, for having worked myself up towards the top of my class. Dropping down, I joined the year below's scholarship form. My father hoped that I would win a scholarship to his former school.

I had been one of the youngest boys in my year, I was now the very oldest in the year below. Through my prep school career, I had showed no talent for any team sports. But now I was larger than the other boys with whom I played football, and at twelve there is little more to the game than the ability to push others off the ball.

I still had friends in the neighbourhood, children who were just preparing to leave their schools a year before me. We continued to spend our afternoons playing football or cricket in the park. One had visions of becoming a professional cricketer. The two of us practised, he bowling to me at a speed which I found alarmingly fast.

At school it was different. Football, having been a chore, became a new-discovered joy. For the first time I was the captain of the teams in which I played. Choosing my own position, I played in midfield or as a striker. In cricket, I tried to teach myself the rudiments of wrist-spin, and did enough albeit at a very slow pace to bamboozle my classmates, many of whom were nine months younger than me.

Cricket pointed the way, indirectly, to my future. At the end of our Wednesday afternoon sessions, I would run from Hyde Park, where the school played its cricket, back to the school itself. A group of us raced the kilometre or so. If any teacher had been watching us, they would hardly have approved, for in our improvised race we chased across busy central London roads. It was simply something we decided to do because we wanted to get back to school, get changed there, and set off home.

In Jimmy's place the title of the fastest boy in the school had passed to a taller boy, Giles, dark-haired, and strong, his skin pitted with acne. A year before, he had shot up and filled out, a sudden early-pubescent growth. I knew from past races that he was faster than me over 50 or 100 metres. But this was a different sort of challenge.

A group of us set off. Within twenty seconds of the start, I was at the front. I ran and ran, refusing to accept that my lungs were short of air. The first week, and each time we ran thereafter, I was invariably the first home.

The school year ended with a sports day, located on the black cinder Duke of York running track, celebrated in athletics history as the place where Roger Bannister had been coached towards breaking the four-minute mile. The track itself was 363 yards long, slightly shorter that is than a standard 400 metre track.

The seriousness of the competition ascended with the age of the children involved. There were egg and spoon race races, relays, jumps. In my first years, the height of my ambition had been to involve my parents in the three legged race. I remember a friend winning one year tied to his father, and the following year coming a forlorn second, his mother's legs tied to his own.

By the time of my last year at school, there were two races which appealed to me: the 100m sprint, and a two-lap race. The winner in the two-lap event won the right to hold briefly a silver champion's plate. I knew my father's history, we had jogged together. He had heard me describe the pleasure of running back to school. I wanted him to be proud of me as an athlete, not just as a boy who wrote.

I wore a white cotton t-shirt and my trainers. There were no distractions when the French teacher raised his starter's pistol in the air. On your marks, set ... go!

I lifted my body from a standing half-crouch and joined the race. Immediately, I was behind. Within half a second of the start, Giles led by two metres. I forced my head back (too far back), my arms and knees forward. My stride lengthened. I strained every muscle I had, I wanted so desperately to win. The end was almost upon me. I reached for it with my chest and arms. I felt the rope of the finishing line around my legs. Giles had already finished four or five metres ahead of me. I finished still further ahead of the boy in third.

I stood by the side of the track afterwards, gasping to fill my lungs with the summer air. My arms were at my hips, I looked down towards the track but I felt no disappointment. I knew my body already. I knew my strengths and some of my weaknesses. I had mentally discounted this defeat before it had happened. The more important battle was yet to come.

It was the two-lap competition on which I focussed. The distance seemed almost inexplicably far. The race's very length was a sign that in the eyes of my school I was now outgrowing my time there. Entering and competing were stages in the ascent from childhood to something closer to adulthood. The key, I had decided, was to get to the inside quickly and lead from the front.

Giles, I was confident, lacked the stamina for the two lap race. But I did not want to be out-sprinted at the finish.

Normally, the start of the 800 metres is run in lanes. This time, we started along a single line. From the gun, I made my way to the front, barging with my shoulder one class-mate attempting the same manoeuvre. From there, it was simply a matter of stretching my legs, at a pace which I thought I could sustain. I measured my lead by the sound, diminishing, of the breathing of the runners behind me. I listened for the spectators, excited at first, then quieter as the gap widened, only stirring again in the last 100 metres or so.

Afterwards my father photographed me, glasses wonky, trophy in hand.

Arriving at my next school, I joined a year of 250 boys, streamed into 14 or so classes and 30 or so "houses". It was a world so large that only those with talent would be noticed. As in any other group of that age, academic success was the least desirable of skills. Some of my contemporaries were superb footballers, cricketers or rowers. Around me there were pupils who would go on to be career footballers, one-day international cricketers, Olympic rowing champions.

In the team sports, I was a worse failure than I had ever been. The standard was higher, my mediocrity was more apparent. Playing for my house second junior team, the ball would spin of my shins as I attempted to trap it. Set up to score, I would manage an air shot. Briefly I tried rugby but I was surrounded by others who had been playing it for up to five years. Rugby sevens without glasses meant I could not even see those that I was supposed to tackle.

I hoped that life would improve in the summer. I told another boy that I would follow my father and choose rowing. As it happened, I was wrong.

I relied on football to keep me fit through the autumn and winter. In some ways, it is not a bad preparation for middle distance running. In an ordinary game, you should be covering something like a good five or six miles, all run in just the very stop-start fashion that is the perfect practice for a 1500 runner's multiple changes of pace.

In the middle of my first term, there was a three-mile cross country race. Enthused by memories of my triumphs at my previous school, but not having trained, I felt sure that I could finish in the top five. I remember little of the competition, save that it had rained and my legs tired beneath the weight of the mud. The longer we raced, the wider were the layers of brown clay stuck to the outsides of my shoes. My feet slid across the ground, my weight lurched forwards and back. I watched in jealousy as other the runners seemed to glide just above the damp, heavy surface.

A red-headed boy Paul won. I finished an unimpressive fortieth, and the other boys in my house teased me afterwards for having dared to think I might do well.

The school held its yearly track and field competition in the spring term. Each pupil had to enter something but we were allowed to choose no more than three events. I opted for the longest races: 400, 800, and 1500 metres. This time I made no predictions. My poor finish in the cross-country meant that none of my friends held any hopes for me. I did try to train a little, but in practice this meant not much more than walking the distance from my house to the field in which the track was located.

The ground was then a cinder track, that is, a surface made up of the deposits left over from burning coal. Unlike the Duke of York track, on which I had raced 12 months before, the cinders were uneven. As we ran, bits of the track would detach themselves. It was far too easy to slip, to sprain an ankle.

A story I heard was that the track had been chewed up once by a well-meaning groundsman's mower. In truth, it could have done with being churned up, watered, and properly flattened. Just a couple of years later, the cinders would be replaced with tartan.

To compete in the 400 metres final, I had to learn skills which I had never considered, such as how to start a race which is only after all an extended sprint. This meant practising crouching at the track, how far to raise my body (only so high) learning how to force myself forward with my arms before my body was fully vertical. As I knew from a year earlier, my start was one of the weakest parts of my race. Watching the other boys, I realised that my finish was little better. I practiced holding my head forwards, sticking my chest out, breaking through the line.

The race itself I began slowly. By 200 metres I had forced my way back to contention but I never quite caught the eventual winner Kris.

In the aftermath of this final, one of the teachers, Charlie, asked me to join the school athletics team. It was not an easy decision, it would mean not following my father into rowing. But here was a skill I had proven already. I had no reason to think I might be half as good in a boat. I asked to sleep on the decision before replying.

My memory of the 1500 metres is that it seemed to start incredibly fast. At 100 metres, I had no greater ambition than to keep up with the runner in second last. And yet, as I overtook him, it did occur to me that I was in less pain than I really should be. I was running against footballers and rugby players of distinction, rather than escaping, they were coming back towards me.

Shortly before the end of the first lap, more in a spirit of playful self-discovery than with any serious plans for the race, I increased my pace towards a sprint. In just a few yards, I brought myself up to fourth. And so the race went on, in alternate periods of recovery and short sprints, until I was second with just a lap to go.

Belatedly, an idea of tactics filtered into my brain. Paul was not in front, but behind. The runner ahead was not someone I could recall from the 400 metres. Suddenly, my body was buzzing with excess energy and I wanted to sprint recklessly. Instead, I made myself check, and check again, and ran to the front only with twenty metres to go.

The 800 metres differs from the 1500 metres. The shorter distance starts in lanes. Runners break in after 150 metres. As they come together, they clash for space on the inside lane. Also, the race is so fast that no runner is capable of more than one change of pace. The knack is to time your finish compared to the people you race.

My rivals in my school 800 metres final included Paul, the cross-country champion, and Kris, who had just beaten me over 400 metres. As we broke from our starting lanes, I found myself jostled, and disturbed by the bodies around me. There was a boy from the year above running immediately behind me. His right leg clipped my trailing foot. He fell forwards, disturbing the runners all around. Wanting to put every possible distance between myself and his fall, I simply sprinted the remaining 600 metres. At each bend, I tucked my weight inwards, scraping a few inches off the total distance. My chest grew tight, my legs tired. Each fifty metres, I had to force myself to accelerate towards the line.

Afterwards, I commiserated the injured runner. Blood streaked down his hands and down his knees.

The Red Vest

In retrospect the Coe-Ovett rivalry divides into three periods: first, for a long period it was no rivalry at all. Ovett was 12 months older than Coe and developed more quickly than him, so that between summer 1974 when Ovett first became an international athlete and summer 1977 when Coe first broke the UK 800 metres record, Ovett was seen as comfortably the top middle-distance runner in Britain.

Then, at its peak, the rivalry was finely balanced. Between, summer 1977 and summer 1981, each runner had a nearly-identical record of winning major championships and of breaking world records. Each could make a decent case to say that they were the fastest middle distance runner in the world.

Finally, from December 1981, when Ovett suffered a first serious injury (he smashed his knee into a set of church railings 200 metres from his home) until the 1984 Olympics, the last occasion when both Coe and Ovett were serious rivals for major honours, Coe was in better shape. Although Ovett was still a good enough runner to break the world 1500 metre record at the end of the 1983 season, he was now prone to injury and in the younger runner's shadow.

Steve Ovett was a recurring presence on my parents' television set. He appeared on A Question of Sport. Then there was an ITV documentary which portrayed his efforts to recover from injury. I saw the bruise on his knee sticking out like a thimble. After the operation, his knee was in plaster for two weeks. There then followed six weeks during which he could not run. He was shown on crutches. So far from being able to resuming training, he was unable even to walk without assistance.

Ovett's father Mick worked at the weekend market in Brighton and even before he had left primary school the future athlete was expected to help him by selling poultry, eggs and meat from the family stall. He spent his school evenings plucking turkeys by the dozen; it was work that left his fingers cracked and sore.

At a young age Ovett had learned a sharp eye for business. There were times when both he and his father cost the family money: the young athlete by selling Christmas turkeys for less than their weight merited, his father in the betting shop. His upbringing taught Ovett to question everyone and everything.

Ovett's mother, Gay, was just 16 years old when her son was born. She ran a market café and later a restaurant and delicatessen. She made the young Ovett the centre of their family life. She cooked for him, cleaned for him, and felt his triumphs just as keenly as he did. For years she played other roles too, as a mentor teaching Ovett to fear no rival and keeping the press at bay. The commentators tried to turn this role on its head by inviting her into their studios so that she and Coe's father Peter could comment on their children's rivalry.

When finally she and Ovett could live in the same house no longer, the mother despairing of his son's engagement with Rachel, who was doing nothing to keep the press away from him, the athlete felt their parting keenly, his face creasing with unwelcome emotion as he attempted to explain his departure.

Ovett's parents' short distance from poverty explains why their son was required to go out and work. Mick and Gay Ovett were not strictly workers but small owners; they employed other people's labour. Yet any capital the family ever owned was borrowed from the banks.

The cameras were in Koblenz, a month after Moscow, to catch Ovett breaking the world 1500 metres record. There were 20,000 people in the stadium standing cheering like a football crowd. Three runners finished inside the old record. When the race ended, the stadium clock initially confused Ovett. He mistook the actual time (3.31) for a less impressive 3.37. Finally grasping that he had broken the record, Ovett grabbed his fellow runners and they ran a victory lap together. Ovett said afterwards that the time was immaterial; he had been focussing on winning the race.

Ovett ran in a red Soviet top that he had swapped with a Soviet athlete Valery Abramov several years before. Rivals complained that by wearing it he was playing up to his image as a rebel. Ovett said he only wore the top because it fitted well.

At the heat of the controversy regarding the Moscow boycott, Ovett let it be known that he had nothing but contempt for Mrs Thatcher. Given the complexion of our national press, that statement was hardly going to win him friends among those who wrote about him. But it did not cause me to think any less of him.

Throughout his running career, Ovett fought a series of battles with authority figures including race promoters and the British Olympic Association as well as the press. From these tussles, he acquired a reputation as conceited. One particular complaint of the press was that Ovett was no team player. In summer 1975, near the start of his international career, Ovett had won the 800 metres at the semi-final of the European Cup. As a result of his and the other athletes' victories Britain qualified for the European Cup final, alongside the athletics superpowers of Poland and Russia. As he had just won the semi-final, it was assumed that Ovett would race in the final itself but, he explained to the press, he did not plan to do so.

The *Daily Mail*'s athletics correspondent Terry O'Connor, a former wartime airman, was outraged that any athlete could decline the honour of representing his or her country. Ovett explained that he was focussed on his own priorities, including not over-exerting himself a year before the Olympics. It was rumoured also that he had plans to watch his girlfriend race.

Ovett was baffled by the thought that other people's patriotism should dictate his running priorities.

Two years later, a further clash occurred when Ovett was blamed for disrupting a Crystal Palace event, organised by the promoter Andy Norman, which was intended to bring together on a single day four of the athletics greats: Ovett, John Walker the Olympic 1500 metres champion, Mike Boit the second-fastest runner in the world over 800 metres, and Alberto Juantorena, Ovett's nemesis from the 1976 Olympics.

The build-up to the event was overtaken by a dual controversy. Originally Juantorena refused to race Boit, the suggestion being that the Cubans did not want to see their champion defeated by a runner who had not been at Montreal. Then, when the organisers proposed to move Boit into Ovett and Walker's race, Ovett refused to agree, saying that he had been contracted to face one and not two world-class rivals. Eventually, the unsatisfactory result was reached that Ovett and Walker would race each other as planned, while Boit and Juantorena ran in two separate 800 metre races.

The newspaper focussed on their own runner's petulance, blaming Ovett entirely, leaving Juantorena out of the picture. "Ovett coward", "Ovett shies away from Boit" and "I blame selfish Ovett" were just a few of the headlines.

Other examples of arrogance were cited against Ovett. Another complaint concerned the habit he developed especially at Crystal Palace, a track where he raced regularly, of waving to the crowd in the closing straight. It was said that he was making fun of the other athletes and that his behaviour showed a lack of respect for the sport. But he was so fast, so much better than his rivals, that the urge to show off must have been irresistible.

A week after Moscow, Ovett was in Crystal Palace, running over 5000 metres against a field which included the former world

3000 metre record holder Brendan Foster. With 100 metres to go, Ovett wearing his red top, pulled out in front, lifting his right arm in celebration, claiming the victory as his. He was soon three metres in front of John Treacy in second. But, as Ovett slowed in the final straight, Treacy ran back at him. I was cheering Ovett even as Treacy dipped first for the line. The race was so close that both he and Ovett were credited with the same time.

"It was a marvellous run", the commentator said, "he won't begrudge Treacy, I'm sure of that."

Ovett was young and ambitious, he like Coe regarded athletics as a business, and he was determined to maximise the financial value of his running career. His running life, as he told interviewers repeatedly, would be short, and he was determined to have as much fun as he could in the limited time available to him. The commercial aspects of Ovett's character were focussed on the practical ends of ensuring a stable but not ostentatious lifestyle for himself and those immediately around him.

Coe and Ovett ran at a time when athletics remained amateur and athletes supposedly could not be paid for their performances. At the start of their careers, they survived, like most of their contemporaries, on the beneficence of a higher education system which enabled them to remain perennial students and paid them grants while they ran. Both chaffed at the limits of amateurism, and by filling stadia they helped to create the mass sporting public from which others built promoters' careers.

By his mid-20s Ovett was running regularly overseas in races where the amateur rules were less closely followed than in Britain. There were rumours that he could command attendance fees of up to £2,000 per race.

Ovett saw amateurism as a sham, as in his words, "an English way of life created to protect the gentleman from the artisan". No doubt this offended some spectators, who preferred Coe's equivocal defence of amateurism as the only way to keep drug cheats out of the sport.

But the real measure of the two athletes is not what they said but what they did and in particular the use that they each put to the tremendous reputation that they had earned by their success at the 1980 Olympics. Ovett devoted his time to founding a running club for Brighton athletes, the Phoenix Athletics Club. It was meant to give a home to the several hundred young athletes who had joined the Brighton and Hove Athletics Club in the aftermath of his victories, but found themselves alone, ignored when they attended the club. Phoenix tried from the outset to give a home to children with the very same abrasive, individual approach to running that Ovett recognised in himself and believed was intrinsic to the sport.

He spent hundreds of hours building up the club. These were hours he might otherwise have spent, like his rival, establishing a career in business.

Beyond his supposed arrogance, the other side of Ovett's running was his superhuman ability to connect with the people who came to the track to watch him run. In August 1981, just ten weeks before his knee injury, Ovett broke the world mile record in Koblenz, again. He was wearing his old Soviet vest, now a pale pink with being so often washed. Through the first two laps the pace was set by a friend of Ovett's, Bob Benn, running in a white UK international top.

For the last 600 metres of the race Ovett ran alone, the crowd willing him forwards all the while. Spectators in their dozens made their way to the outside lanes of the track. The whole stadium was applauding in unison and chanting his name, and when he finished and lifted his arms there were hundreds of people on the track to cheer. Coe, who broke many more records than Ovett, never generated quite the same response from his crowds.

Far from disliking Ovett for his abrasiveness or pride, it seems more accurate to say that his audience – who were overwhelmingly young and working-class – saw in his battles with authority something of their own lives.

Injured

On joining the school athletics team, I was introduced to some of the apparatus of track running. I was encouraged to buy a pair of spiked running shoes, and I opted for the lightest pair, grey, with barely any support in the heels. I bought different sizes of spikes, 6mm for tartan, 15mm for cinders. No doubt, they would have been ideal for a sprinter. But with the 15mm spikes on, it was like wearing a set of high heels in reverse; my achilles was shortened, my heel rested on the ground below my toes.

I bought a top and socks in the team's colours of deep burgundy. I purchased my first lycra shorts and more robust training shoes.

I learned how to train, properly. The essence of this was to do nothing until your body was properly limbered up. I acquired a 15-minute warm up, which I still practise: stretching first my neck then my shoulders, my back and hips, then my upper legs, and finally my calves. Just as important, it was drummed into us, was to warm down gradually always after any exercise, by repeating the same stretches. We were then encouraged to jog gently back home.

Charlie's philosophy of running was simple. There was no better way he said to build up fitness than by running short distances at a high intensity. Sometimes, we would build up from 100 metre sprints, with a short recovery, to 200m, 300m, 400m and so on. At other times we would race in repeated 200-metre or 400-metre bursts.

I was never encouraged to train anything less than flat-out. I would run with the fastest boys who were two or three years older than me. I delighted in the feeling that I could keep up with them, if briefly. Soon I was training three evenings a week, racing twice during the week, and then once again at weekends. An ordinary inter-school competition would comprise 800m and 1500m races and often also relays. I was getting faster and taking seconds off my best times whenever I ran.

On the return from the track one Thursday afternoon, I found myself passing one of the team's sprinters, Adam. He asked if I had been training, and I said yes, of course. "You run every day, don't you?" he asked. "Yes." "Don't overdo it." It was advice that I would have done better to follow.

I remember racing the school's 200 metre champion over a trial distance of 400 metres. It was his suggestion, a distance at what he had identified as the midway point between our rival strengths. After 100 metres, he led me by 15 yards. Tall, powerful, he was not merely fast, he was stretching away from me. Towards the end of the back straight however, his body seemed to seize up. By 200 metres, I was upon him, and we could almost touch. By 250 metres, I was definitely ahead. At 300 metres, he simply stopped. He looked horrified, as I turned, shouted back at him and urged him to finish the race.

A 100-metre sprinter barely needs to breathe; their success will depend altogether on the volume of fast twitch muscles in their body. These muscles produce lactic acid, which will eventually force the sprinter to stop, but the oxygen debt is not felt until around 300 metres (this is one reason why you so often see 400 metre runners gasping for oxygen at the end of a race).

A middle distance runner by contrast relies on transferring oxygen to the muscles so that the sprinter's "wall" is never reached.

The first time I ran for the school, I guessed that the competition would be more taxing than anything I had faced. I assumed that I would finish last. Later in the day, having won both the 800 and 1500 metres, I began to relax. At my second inter-school meet I came across Jimmy, who had been so much faster than me two years before. We had to race 800 metres heats, then a final. He did not even make it through to the final.

My new feeling of invincibility extended to schools I had not yet raced. At a third event we entered a medley relay: two sprinters running 200 metres each, a 400-metre lap, and then me over 800 metres. I was becoming cocky. My view was that provided none of the other runners had more than a 50 metres head start on me, our team would win.

I was getting close to the school record for 800 metres. Yet from time to time a runner at another school might beat me over that distance. Over 1500 metres, by the end of the season, I had not lost. I had not found a runner who could beat me.

Midway through the season, I was training at close to maximum pace. Sprinting round a bend, I felt an unexpected pain low in my left calf. Racing on, the pain intensified. Even after I had slowed, my leg remained sore. Taking my shoe off afterwards, I could see that the skin around my left tendon was swollen. For a week I did not run, wrapping my leg in a shop-bought bandage. The injury remained.

Seen from behind, a healthy lower leg has something of an hourglass shape. The calf is a great mass of muscle at the top. The leg then narrows as you look down it, the achilles tendon is often very thin. As you reach the ankle, the leg flares out again. Injured, my left leg lacked this narrow shape. Between the muscle and the bone, the tendon was shortened and wide.

My amateur attempts to mend my body did little good. The school doctor showed me how after a week of wearing the bandage my left calf was three inches thinner than my right. He treated me with an ancient metal ultrasound box running on clockwork. After two weeks of treatment, he encouraged me to run again.

I spent a weekend with my parents in the country house which had once been my grandparents' home. Looking through the tall chest in the main living room, I found among letters and other documents a black book with a red spine. It was my father's university diary, in parts of it he looked back on his days at the same school where I now studied. He let me keep the diary; I would read it carefully later.

Returning to fitness, I had a couple of weeks of the season left. At another race at the Oxford University track, I was just a little slower than I had been prior to my injury. I was feeling my body back to fitness and did not dare relax fully. I asked Charlie if I could be protected in future from having to run 800m and 1500m races on the same day. Better advice might have been to run but not always at top speed.

In the second competition, I timed 2.12.1 for 800 metres, breaking the school's under-15 record. The following week my time had been placed, with the other records, on the noticeboard in the hut beside the school athletics track.

A Real Racer Who Never Tires

My grandfather was gentle and kind. He played cricket, football and rugby for his college and came first in the Oxford cross country race. He grew up in the shade of his elder brother Noel, who was killed in the first year of the war of 1914-1918. Four-fifths of his regiment died or were incapacitated in a fatal charge.

My grandmother too was over-shadowed in her youth. Blind in an eye after an early accident, she was eclipsed by her older sister, the discoverer of hidden oases in the North African desert, a friend of Mussolini and of the Queen, a celebrity in interwar England. My grandmother was my grandfather's second wife; she married him only after his first wife, her own best friend Meg, had died in childbirth.

Years later, my grandmother wrote to my father, describing his birth. My grandfather was summoned from work, returning home to meet his son. Blissfully content, rather sleepy, my grandmother looked with surprise at her wriggling, slightly comic, roly-poly child. She knew her son would suffer moments of pain and disappointment, because everybody must know a little sadness. But she wanted him to love everything, and to be alive every single minute.

By the start of the Second World War, my father was still just nine-years-old. He had a handsome face, an easy manner and a levelling humour. One spring he and his younger brother built themselves two pairs of stilts, practising as if they were training for the circus. Another year, they found a deserted raft. The boys watched the German and the British aircraft fighting through the night. In term-time they were sent to boarding school, twice the house was bombed, the boys missing the excitement.

My father's first diaries, made from paper torn from a school book, record private and public triumphs: Soviet advances on captured towns, Allied victories on all fronts, a Christmas dinner of turkey, plum pudding, chocolate and Turkish delight, a birthday gift of a tennis racket, and the very grand gift of a full £3 to spend.

Too many people were grumbling, he warned. The worst form of grumbling was about money in factories. People were grumbling at trifles and hindering the war effort. Dissension was especially among miners who strike and caused less coal to be sent to the factories. Do the troops strike, he asked rhetorically, wouldn't it be awful if they did?

My grandfather was serving now in the intelligence corps. One of his duties was to interview citizens of the Axis powers who were refugees in Britain, separating those who were to be treated as potential spies from those to be treated as loyal subjects. Later my grandfather served away from London, spiriting agents behind German lines in Corsica, and was away from home for months on end. His letters tell of meals in "country pubs", of bathing in seas unnamed.

By late summer of his final year of preparatory school, my father was eager for sports day, having qualified for the 100 yards, 440 yards hurdles and long jump finals, although in the end he was unable to compete, having come down the day before with a sudden flu. "I spent my sports day in bed. I let my imagination win everything!" He spent the holidays preparing for the transition to his pending school by practising rowing at Regent's and Battersea parks.

My grandfather approved my father's interest, "I do wonder how you will like it. I believe that when a boat is going really well and everybody is rowing really well together then there is the most marvellous thrill."

On his arrival at his new school in early September, my father was 13-years-old. The pupils lived in large houses, dominated by a troika of house master, dame and house captain. The latter, generally a senior boy remaining at school in the hope of being taken on at Oxford or Cambridge, was in charge of discipline. A book recorded his memories of the year, guidance for the incoming house captain.

The Dame ensured the boys were fed and received basic medical care. My father's Dame was a Mrs Walker, of whom an outgoing house captain recorded, "She could be very nice but she had no idea at all of how to look after boys."

My father's house masters were successively a Mr Rowlatt and a Mr Parr. Rowlatt was known as "Tin Tummy", for the injuries he had incurred during the previous war. Parr was called "Purple Parr". Parr "is very pompous", one of his house captains noted, "and can only treat one as a human being with a great effort." Parr caused a modest scandal by marrying a Mrs Murphy and acquiring four Catholic children. These were extra mouths to be fed, it was hinted, from the boys' budget.

Outside the school, men were distinguished by military rank; hierarchy could be recognised in the badges that adorned an officer's lapel. So it was in the house, some of the oldest boys were prefects in Debate, others in Library. The boys in Debate could order the youngest pupils to run errands ("fag") for them. A member of Debate would shout "boy" and the juniors would come running. The last to arrive would be sent off to deliver the message, or whatever it was they were being asked to do.

Had the system been challenged, it would have been said that it was not frivolous but was linked to the circumstances of war. Boys were required to serve in the school's training corps, learning the rudiments of marching and target practice. "Most people seem to dislike the Corps intensely", one of my father's contemporaries wrote, "Of course, if treated as a nuisance, it rapidly becomes so."

Some senior boys worked on Sundays in a nearby factory,

while others doubled up as air raid messengers or were asked to guard against the menace of fire bombs. Summer afternoons were broken up as boys were sent off to contribute to various harvest camps.

My father was tall for his age and slender but his shoulders and arms were strong. In photographs, his right eye seems wider open than his left. He appears handsome, and quite relaxed. His face formed easily into a wry smile. Yet, happy as he seems in the photographs, I gather that my father's first months at the new school were no fun at all. Three other boys arrived with him. Two of them were older and had just been repatriated from Canada to England. He ate alone.

His house captain recorded, in an unenthusiastic note to the housemaster, the arrival of the four new pupils. With my father, the arrivals were "Huntington, Gasden, C. Cory, all of them seem to be pleasant and keen, but not outstanding".

My father read widely, losing himself in Joseph Conrad's novels of the sea, but he was not in the school's top classes. He was average at Latin and Greek, he did better at maths. In his last three years, he even had to endure the presence of a younger brother. The brother was a scholar and as such was placed straight into the Upper School, that is, the year above my father.

My father's school contemporaries, like mine would later, placed a heavy emphasis on sporting ability. To be known in the school, you had to excel at something. The house captain recorded my father's performance in the school athletics competition, "He ran well but did not reach the final of anything". My father's best race, I gather was the 880 yards (by my time, of course, the 800 metres). His body had seen a subtle development of stamina compared to his favourite running events twelve months earlier, the 100m and the 400m hurdles.

In the house half mile, "Macpherson ma and Huitfeldt drew

for 1st place after a very hard race." My father was third. The first real signs of development came in the summer, when my father chose rowing over cricket or athletics, fulfilling the plans he had previously discussed with my grandfather. My father took quickly to rowing, finding his balance easily in the boat and acquiring a natural rhythm. He reached the final of the first year sculling, his house captain recording, "A good effort!"

My father developed as a rower, and continued to run in the following spring. He even represented the school, occasionally, in half-mile races.

The school had a fixed routine for teaching new boys to row. The first stage was a swimming test. Once a boy could swim 100 metres or so, they would go to the boathouse "Rafters" and be placed in a clinker skiff, and from there they built up slowly to sculling boats with first fixed and then sliding seats. Rowlatt did not teach his junior boys to row, instead, another teacher Connybeare was in charge of the Rowlatt junior scullers. Towards the end of the summer, to show them how it was done properly, he drove the boys over to Henley to watch the Regatta.

As they floated down Henley Hill, Connybeare stopped the engine to save fuel, "Go on, go on..." he would shout, as the car descended, restarting the engine as they reached the next hill. My father imagined Connybeare among the other teachers reaching into his coat, and holding his hand over his heart, "go on, go on..."

My father was passed over for the junior eights, and spent his summers sculling by himself. Largely untaught, but enjoying the exercise, he found himself slowly building up his distance until he was rowing dozens of miles every week.

No amount of practice could have prepared my father for his first weeks rowing on the river. He would have been surrounded by dozens of other boys, also learning to row. Amongst the beginners will have been boys whose boats twisted first one and then the other, boys who lacked the strength or technique to row against a current, boys rowing without finesse their oars flapping on and against the water. Several no doubt will have capsized as they struggled to cope with the wash of steamers boating over from Windsor. The best of the new intake must surely have done little more than paddle themselves gently away from the worst beginners.

Step by step, my father will have learned to coordinate the kick in his legs and the thrust in his arms, where to place his energy, how to hold his hands around the oars. He must have learned to trust his body to come forward (too far forward, it will once have seemed) at the start of the stroke, and to fall back far (too far?) at its end.

He breathed the fresh summer air. He returned to his house afterwards, his face red from the sun, content.

At the end of the stroke, the body is upright and the legs flat out and the arms by the body with the top end of the oars close to the body. A slight twist of the wrist brings the oars out of the water and into a flat position. The rower must then balance forward putting his weight firmly onto his feet. Doing this successfully enables the forward movement to take place without the boat slipping to one side.

The sculler swings fully forward getting his sculls as far back as he can with his arms flat out forward. The sculls are entered into the water with a flick of the wrist. He must simultaneously push his weight on his legs as quickly as he can. If the entry into the water is slow the boat will be temporarily stopped. Half way through the stroke the rower swings his body back and finally pulls the oars close to the body.

Sculling on the Tideway has particular problems because of the floating debris at high tide. When the river is high, waves also rock the boat as they bounce off the tidal walls. This makes balancing the boat very hard.

Around my father's sixteenth birthday, five of the boys in his house "were discovered in a degrading juvenile act." Their punishments ranged from admonishment, demotion from their positions in Debate, to (for the most junior boys) a thrashing.

Scandals in the house continued. Rumours reached the Library that a boy in my father's year "had a motorbicycle in the High Street and not infrequently used it." The boy in question was told by the house captain, "that if this was true or not he must clearly understand that if he was discovered in any affair of this kind he could not remain in the school." Afterwards, the house master "discovered another affair which assumed the very blackest proportions when" another of my father's contemporaries "refused to tell the truth, attempted to hoodwink M'Tutor and deliberately deceived his own father." There was a reason for the lies, the first boy "had been found by a police constable riding a motorbicycle, without a licence, which belonged to" the second. The two boys were both duly expelled.

This was a time before cars were common, and a motorbike represented freedom. My father would request a bike of his own for his next birthday.

An extract from the school rules gives a sense of how many prohibitions there were, "Boys are forbidden to enter Theatres of Cinemas, to visit Race Courses, or enter the shops of Tobacconists or Pawnbrokers. Boys are forbidden to enter any Railway Station, Hotel, Public House, Private House, House Boat or Launch without their House Master's leave." The references to boats and launches could hardly have been accidental, the river, like a train, was an escape from watching eyes.

At seventeen, my father won the school's junior sculls. Immediately after, he raced in the senior sculls, coming second against boys a year older than him. At one key moment, he found himself in direct competition with a rower in the school's first eight. My father, to his own astonishment, passed the senior boy without difficulty. He was promoted immediately to the school's first eight. He had never rowed consistently in an eight before.

My father's explanation for this breakthrough is that through years of sculling by himself he had developed a decent technique. The people he was racing had spent years in junior or upper eights. Without planning it, he was simply better prepared as a sculler than they were.

Anyone who learns to row must begin by sculling on their own, later, as they grow in confidence, they may be invited to join other rowers in an eight. Rowing is a unique team sport in that all the members of the collective are right at the heart of the action. If any of them falters, the whole boat slows down at once.

Learning to row as part of a collective is a brutal and tiring activity. I think of my father, his hamstrings and back aching, his legs short of strength, his head light and struggling to breathe. Overworked, trying so desperately to maintain his technique, he like every member of the eight would have felt a temptation to let their effort ease. Rowing requires not merely cardiovascular fitness but absolute determination to push through the pain barriers which hit, one after another.

The inevitable lesson would have been absorbed, that strength and power alone are not enough to make a boat go quickly. A boat's pace should be steady, his coaches must have told him, like the beating of a heart. Rhythm happens when stroke and recovery are co-ordinated, when the oars and the boat are as one.

My father was still seventeen, the winter was cold. Pupils wore thick coats and held their arms close to their bodies. One day, he watched a groundsman flood one of the fields with water. Two days later, a frost came, and the boys placed ice hockey on the frozen surface. Soon, snow lay thick on the ground. The outdoor toilets froze and the boys were sent home.

On the first day of spring, a sly, meretricious downpour cleared the remaining ice. The rains, welcomed when they came, continued. On they went, until the ground was a sponge crying to be wrung out. Where usually the Thames was flat, now it ran fast and loud. The river broke its banks. Trees were thrown down, paths ran like flowing silver. Sandbags were built into temporary barricades in front of low-lying homes. Those living by the river evacuated their possessions. In some cases, buildings were ruined, their facades torn off. Whole banks of earth on which train lines had once stood were washed away, leaving iron struts suspended in mid-air. Demobilised soldiers were to be seen digging silt from their flooded homes.

Everywhere could be seen the efforts of building, cleaning and drying.

At eighteen, my father won the school's senior sculls from Christopher Davidge. "In the earlier stages the final was a fine race", the school newspaper reported "After a false start Davidge took the lead. At Brocas Clump he went across too violently." My father picked up the pace as Davidge stalled, gaining the inside of the bend, "Davidge did not allow him to rest, and the distance between them remained about two lengths until the ryepeck." Downstream, my father increased his lead slightly. "Davidge closed up a little at Hester's Shed", but my father rowed away to win by three lengths. Davidge and my father would later row together for Oxford.

The same summer, my father was part of an eight which won the Ladies Plate at Henley, beating the eights of several Oxford and Cambridge colleges (Brasenose, Clare, and Lady Margaret) as well as the eights of various other schools. In a race to the barrier (a two minute sprint), my father's eight also beat Leander Club, who would represent England at that year's Olympics.

My father, his house captain recorded "rowed magnificently at 3. He is a real racer who never tires and really enjoys the damned sport."

That July's Henley regatta was dominated by the prospect of the pending Olympic regatta, which was due to be raced on the same course just four weeks later. Trials for the Olympics had already taken place, and several Olympians were due to compete at Henley, including the eventual gold medal winners in the coxless pairs and double sculls. The composition of the Leander Olympic eight was already determined, giving younger rowers every reason to test themselves against them.

Leander made the Olympic final, where they were faced with an American eight, the inheritor of three decades of US supremacy in the event.

The eventual American triumph was duly added by the press to Britain's long history of actual defeats and stirring near-victories, "The machine-like precision and superior strength of the United States gradually wore down the young British crew of undergraduates", *the Times* explained, "The Americans were rhythmic and powerful and won handsomely." Britain's golds came elsewhere. The coxless pairs was won by a pair of former Cambridge undergraduates who had barely trained together in a decade, both had been in the Sudan, where one had been seriously injured by a spear. Their first race together was the Olympic trial.

My father's hands were calloused and his body ached. Five years of steady improvement as a rower had taken him to an achievement that no previous group of schoolboy rowers had matched in more than a decade. In front of him, my father had fourteen months' national service before he began at Oxford. I see him setting off from the train station with a group of other junior officers from similar backgrounds. Ahead of them are drills, classes, and weapons training. Three months will be spent in the company of rank-and-file soldiers, men whose lack of formal education prevents them from becoming officers, but who hold the advantage over their leaders in that they have spent several years in actual conflict, in contrast to these young, over-promoted boys. The trainee officers are nervous to see what awaits them; my father breaks the common anxiety by telling a lengthy and probably obscene joke.

My father's younger brother was left behind at school.

During his last few weeks before national service, my father made best use of his new motorbike. On his departure, following an accident on an Essex country lane, my grandmother determined that the bike would have to be sold.

At school, my father had been trained in the British tradition of scepticism and empiricism. His views, and the views of his friends, were the views they had picked up loyally from their parents' generation. He had learned from the war to associate ideas with vile dictators and their obedient followers. But if any sport was a Hegelian paradigm it was rowing. Here, to a greater extent than in football, in rugby, cricket or certainly in athletics, the team was capable of no greater triumph than could be managed by its weakest part. Individualism offered little, conformity in the search for a shared pace was all. The coxless pairs might be won by the perfect combination of two surprisingly matched amateurs but eights' rowing was a matter of combining a group, rowers working together beyond the limits of pain.

Subtly, and not without conflict, a different way of experiencing life was seeping into my father's skin. He was learning to think beyond his parents' views.

The university he would join was more sceptical in its thinking even than my father. Given the limitations of his class and generation, my father was inching towards the most collective philosophy available to him.

1.59.7

Why did I run? I ran because it was there. Only once in my youth did I see the possibility of success at any other sport. Aged 12, my school gym teacher constructed a simple high jump frame, and attempted to teach our class the first rudiments of a Frosbury flop. We took turns to jump, and as those who could clear the hurdle continued the bar was raised, in increments, to four feet and even higher. The sport came to me naturally. For the last six jumps, all but the first of which I cleared at the first opportunity, I jumped alone.

Surprised, for I was no natural at any other sport, the teacher then attempted to repeat the competition the following day. I tried to jump three feet, that is, some 12 inches lower than I had managed the day before. Having failed twice, I could jump no more. I did not have the confidence to go on. I lacked the character as a jumper to continue.

Running was different. It came to me intuitively and represented little of a challenge. I could not comprehend those who were incapable of running 100 metres in 13 seconds or less.

My school contemporaries were vacuous with the confidence of people who at the ages of thirteen or fourteen had never once been hungry or known others in hunger. Their heroes were in our ruling party, then engaged in the privatising of our public utilities, the dismantling of the welfare state, the making of the right conditions so that the rich would never again pay but the minimum of taxes.

The other boys had the security of parents' incomes rooted in banking and finance. My background was little different but unlike most of my year, I had no trust fund. In addition, growing up in a family where politics was discussed nightly, I had watched the news of the steel-workers and then the miners' strikes, willing the workers to succeed against our leaders who seemed to delight in their humiliation.

Endlessly expressing the narrowness of our existence and our isolation from what 99 percent of people considered life, I bored my contemporaries by pointing out their isolation until they had no more desire to speak to me than I had to them. My hero was another boy, Gobber, who took to a tall building and spat on his fellow pupils repeatedly.

School assemblies brought speakers lecturing us on our superiority. Cabinet ministers came to speak, as did top generals, ambassadors, heads of charities, the executives of top businesses. They spoke with a constant refrain: "You are the brightest and the best." The brightest? I thought of the look of slow-dawning horror on one friend's face after he was presented with a pair of motorcycle boots for his sixteenth birthday, and over the next half-hour it became apparent that he would be unable to fit them onto his feet. The best? This was a cohort incapable of the least sympathy for the weak or the poor.

I could not fight everybody. Running, a strategy cohered. I read, more widely than the school's resources allowed. Away from its environment, I voiced plans to run away and watched the reactions of those on whom I tried them out, chiefly, my horrified parents. I learned to plan a different programme, one that might not be fulfilled for several years to come. I studied hard; I wrote.

The two wheels of my public life and my internal universe were turning at very different speeds. The cog that joined them was my running. It kept me well.

I ran also to maintain a bond with my father. I knew that he had wanted a son who would follow him, who would take over his businesses and the houses in which he had lived, who would direct the family's affairs, who would offer succeeding generations the same guarantees against poverty that he had given me. He complained to his friends that I wanted to level down people. He was upset that we did not share any interests, that there was nothing in his life we could enjoy together. My parents disliked my politics, my clothes and diet, almost everything they saw in me. They were chided in their turn for allowing me to think differently. "Your son is a vegetarian", another parent told my father, "if my son came home and wouldn't eat meat, I'd starve him until he agreed." The words were spoken quite seriously.

When I returned home during the holidays to the family dining table, I found that the range of topics we could happily discuss was on each visit narrowed.

By running, and at a high standard, I hoped to gain at least a temporary forgiveness from my father for my many other failings.

In my second year of school athletics I reduced my 800 metres personal best by five seconds, and my 1500 metres time by 15 seconds. I mentored the youngest members of the team, guiding them into the habits of training. I relaxed into my running, allowing my brain to clear, leaving me focussed on my body. I could blot out the wind, all sounds of people around me. I would concentrate on my breathing, making sure that my lungs were filled as deeply as I could with air.

In my third year I won the school's under-17 800 metres and 1500 metres. The first two-thirds of the season I lost however to a further injury.

I could sense the injuries to my achilles tendon before they happened. My left leg would stiffen. There was a subtle cumulative difference between the ordinary fatigue that was a necessary part of challenging myself to run fast, and the intense pain of a joint that was damaged beyond immediate recovery. Injured, it felt as if someone had painted a sore red line horizontally across the tendon, at the mid-point of my left ankle joint. I felt increasingly jaded and was looking for something new.

On my eventual return from injury, I raced in the local county championships. The first surprise was that the boys' and girls' 800 metres finals were being run together; this was the first time I had had to run against women. The second surprise was that the competitors all ran hard from the start. In the inter-schools events, all athletes had raced each other several times, and knew well our strengths and weaknesses. We often had a negative split in the 800m, with the second lap faster than the first. The racing was cagey, the best runners waited to sprint at the end.

It was nothing like that in the county championship; I set off at a mediocre 32 seconds for the first 200 metres. I was immediately at the back of the field, behind not just every boy in the race, but every girl too. I couldn't understand why the athletes at the front were running 25 seconds at the start; only international athletes could maintain that sort of pace. The other runners weren't that fast were they?

At each 100 metre interval thereafter, I found myself overtaking small knots of runners who had simply set off too fast.

I passed the last of the girls, a second girl, then a boy and another girl. At the halfway point, I was still down in fourth. "Sixty-four, sixty-five", I could hear the marshals calling out as I neared the bell. The field was stretched out, and the leader was still around 50 metres ahead. I had no expectation at all of challenging him. All I knew was that my body felt relaxed. Yet after my break for injury I felt under-raced. Why not give it a go? I thought.

Over the next 200 metres, I clawed back around half the lead, and was soon placed in second. My chest was high as I raced, my fingers outstretched. My arms and hands pumped up and down. I passed the former leader 50 metres from the line, his chest upright, his head way back over his toes.

My 200 metre splits were I estimate 32-32-28-29; his splits I guess were 25-31-32-35. He must have been in agony, trying to will his body forward when it had nothing left to give. By contrast, I felt ecstatic. Had I been asked to start a second race immediately afterwards, I would happily have done so.

Immediately after the race a man introduced himself to me. Joe had the features of a dressed turkey, albeit with a shorter neck; he was plump, overweight, and had no hair on his head but a drinker's maroon nose. Do you have a coach, he asked? I did already, I explained. Would you like a new one? I did not agree straightaway but agreed to take his details; I disliked the school and was fed up with both the team and the training.

Joe gave me a view of a much more serious world of track racing. I started to train in the evenings with his group, mainly through gentle 6- or 8-mile runs. His group comprised a large number of youthful waifs and strays picked up from local schools. There were several runners in his entourage who had been selected as youth internationals. His daughter, I learned, was a senior international.

Joe encouraged me to race the following week in an open event being run on a nearby track. That would mean running against athletes of all ages, a point Joe forgot to explain to me. If he had, I do not know if I would have dared enter.

The event was cursed once again by athletes, this time in their mid-twenties, setting a pace I could not match. Trying to keep up with the front group, I managed a first lap of 52 seconds, not much slower than my best 400m pace. Staring at the necks of the runners in front of me, willing myself with every force in my possession to follow them, I compelled myself to keep up, as best I could, with the runners ahead.

I slowed in the third quarter, found myself running in a group of one, and slowed again towards the end. In the final straight, I could barely keep going. My head lolled from side to side, and my stride was without rhythm. I must have finished fifth or worse out of 12. Yet when I saw the clock, I realised that I had managed something special. My time was 1.59.7, under two minutes for the half mile. I was well inside the school record, and a full second within my personal best.

I was delighted, if a week of a new coach could shave seconds off my best time, how much better would I run after a proper pre-season training?

There was no time to bask in my success, the season was not yet finished. I had been asked by Charlie to run in our inter-schools' 800 metres final, the last race of the season. I looked at the competition record and saw that the fastest time in the competition's history was just over two minutes, slower, that is, than I had just run. I felt as fit as I had ever been. I boasted to select friends that I had every chance of victory.

Spending a weekend at my parents', practising snooker, I noticed that my cue tip was worn. I prepared a replacement, smoothing it with sandpaper. Dust entered my lungs. The next morning, I was coughing. The day after, my chest went into spasms. The doctor tested my lung capacity, comparing it unfavourably with that of a 70 year old's. But if I routinely breathed in less air than most of my contemporaries, how could I run?

After ten days of inhalers, the mucus in my lungs began to fade from brown to green, but still breathing weakly, I could not train. I finished in a demoralising fourth. The medallists were runners I had beaten repeatedly before.

My Father's Diary

Now a student, my father rowed for Oxford in the boat race. The BBC sent almost every camera in the Corporation's possession to film the race, giving it better coverage that almost any other event, sporting or political, in the year.

On leaving school, my father had kept up his sports, after a fashion. He attempted to run the hurdles for the Guards, injuring himself in the process. Before starting at Oxford, he had rowed in a four for his future college. When he arrived at Oxford, he was immediately around the edges of the boat race crew, rowing every afternoon without exception.

The President of the Oxford boat, and its intended stroke (the rower who sets the pace) was Christopher Davidge, my father's former school rival. Apart from Davidge, most of the previous eight had ended their studies, and a new boat had to be found with places for four other of my father's school contemporaries. My father himself was in and out of the boat, until finally picked by a coach who had seen him row at Henley. Days before the race, Oxford suffered a decisive blow, Davidge was struck down by jaundice and had to be replaced.

By 10am, the *Evening Standard* reported, "crowds of Cup Final size were jostling through Hammersmith, Chiswick, Putney and Mortlake." Oxford chose the Surrey station. They led at the start, and the crews were still level after a mile, but Cambridge drew ahead in the second mile. At Hammersmith Bridge, Oxford had the bend in their favour and reduced Cambridge's lead. I imagine my father, already near the very limits of his strength, trying to increase the power of his stroke. He had to find more energy when his body was already near its fastest pace, yet he could not row with too much force for fear of disrupting the other rowers in his own boat.

Oxford increased their pace to a punishing 34 strokes per minute, Cambridge however had the benefit of the bend at the Middlesex station. Cambridge were ahead, but erratic steering by their cox brought them close to the Oxford boat, and for a brief moment the two crews' oars touched before separating again.

As the river straightened, Cambridge remained in the lead and Oxford could not wear their rivals down. Slowly, Cambridge's lead mounted. They eventually rowed out winners by the comfortable margin of three-and-a-half lengths.

My father's diary begins six months after Oxford's defeat: "It is given to undergraduates and those of that age in particular", it starts, "to ask what is the point. Afterwards a middle-aged smugness settles in combined with a feeling of having lost something. This causes such expressions from the old – 'how lucky you are to be young.' There we are with our chance all over to do something worthwhile but 99% of us are destined to stamp on the desire to do something worthwhile for the sake of marriage and so curing our loneliness or for money or security or fear or something."

"The result is that we forget that in our youth we used to despise the prospect of the bowler hat, the city train, *the Financial Times*, the grey-haired wife and sticky children. Perhaps we will consider ourselves wiser then, maybe we will be. But as it is we do not have the courage to be a monk, or the conviction to be a politician. We drift. And we try to convince ourselves that what we are doing is worthwhile."

Over the next few years, the diary records my father's protracted attempts to give meaning to his life.

My father turned against the realisation that he was fated to live in a particular area of the country, doing a particular kind of job and would live in no other way. Meaning, or in my father's language, "faith", was seen by him as the necessary adoption of irrational belief. The choices were limited: a convert might determine, "that the hand of God can be seen in everything good and that he minutely controls our destinies, that the Fuhrer is always right, that Marx as interpreted by Lenin and Stalin is infallible, that the followers of Mahommed will go straight to heaven if they die in battle". Of these four options, only the first had any attraction, and even then its appeal was initially limited.

My father was shaped by an intellectual culture which praised those who broke down belief systems, not those who joined them. "If a faith demanded my physical compliance, if it demanded fasting or that one should cease the athletic cult of one's body one would not worry, in fact it would be an extra homage on the altar. But if it demands intellectual surrender, one retracts."

He was showing every sign of dissatisfaction with disbelief.

My father needed solid ground from which to judge the moral choices open to him. He noted in his diary eight moments of unequivocal pleasure:

1. Sculling in the sun. (note not at Oxford)
2. Winning the Ladies Plate.
3. Shooting in the early morning at Folly Mill.
4. Autumn mornings particularly the ones in which one's breath can be seen. Winter fires and the list tails off: I leave out childhood ones, they are too bound up with sentiment; and no recent ones have yet gathered real force. But the start of the recent list seems to be something like.
5. High Mass, always especially the Credo.
6. Driving back to Oxford at 6 am.
7. Certain mornings in G- St. but again I am not sure of that. The Chartreusian monastery and certain things of beauty

in the sun, but always the detail never the whole.

8. Walking down the Mall to St James' barracks underneath the rather odd lights there, all in a straight row.

Folly Mill was my grandparents' home in Essex. St James' barracks was where my father had done his national service with the Guards'. The dislike of Oxford rowing is harder to explain.

My best guess is as follows, when he had first taken up rowing, at around the age of fourteen, my father was at a boarding school. His immediate environment was one of restraint. His classes were in the same buildings. On finishing lessons, he was supposed to return to his house, where rotas were checked each evening to make sure that the whereabouts of all the boys were known. The school was not far from London, many of the boys (as indeed my father) had grown up in the city, and were used to the wider possibilities of urban life. Structured into the fabric of school life was the idea that pupils, as they got older, were supposed to have greater freedom. That possibility would have been closed off, by necessity, during the war.

As a schoolboy, it follows, rowing was a means to freedom. It released my father's body; it took him to places he would not otherwise have seen.

As a student, rowing was a restraint. It took my father away from pleasures which were not otherwise restricted. It kept him from books, from religion, and from romance. In time, even the thrill of competition must have paled.

The Grimace

I had turned against Coe and refused to return to him, even during 1981, the year which both runners later identified as the best of their careers. It produced four world records over 800 metres, 1500 metres or the mile. Coe claimed three of the records, including the last, the record for the mile, which he achieved pulling away from Mike Boit in Brussels at the end of August.

There was something wilful about my choice, it put me at odds not merely with my father and the other children at school who followed the sport, but also informed opinion among journalists both on television and in the press. Coe was regarded by all experts as a superior athlete.

When he ran, I admit, he was sometimes extraordinary. In Brussels, he beat John Walker (his predecessor as Olympic 1500 metre champion) by more than a hundred metres. Boit's time coming second in the race was good enough to make him the fifth-fastest miler of all time. Coe managed all this despite striking his foot mid-race on the metal sleeve marking the inside of the track. But I could not force the same admiration for him that I had for Ovett.

I saw in the newspapers the photograph of Coe as he breaks the finishing line at the end of the 1500 metres at Moscow. He stands straight, with arms to each side, his upper body in a crucifixion pose. His head is pulled backwards, and the muscles at the front of his neck are tight. Every muscle in his face is pulled up, away from his neck. His mouth widens in a grimace. Even his brows are arched. I studied that image at the time and have looked it again many times since. I saw no pleasure in it then and find none today.

It is not a look of ecstasy; it shares nothing with the much simpler images of Ovett after his gold at Moscow: a clenched fist, the search for a particular face in the crowd, a smile. Indeed in all the images of Ovett racing I can see only familiar emotions: fatigue, elation, desire, the anger of defeat, the joy of success.

Coe's grimace was one of those rare occasions when he allowed his deepest emotions to rise to the surface. What it shows very clearly is that he ran not in pleasure but chiefly in fear.

Seb Coe, like Steve Ovett, grew up in a family dominated by a strong central figure. In Coe's case it was his father Peter, a factory manager. A Channel Four documentary, shown just in time for the Los Angeles Olympics, opened with Peter Coe in a silver anorak and outsize glasses telling the story of Coe's running career: "At 14 I really thought he was good, and at 16 I was certain that if I was patient and played it right he would be a world beater." Peter Coe pronounced the word cer-ta-in with a slow, lumbering manner, turning two syllables into three.

By 1984, I had my own working television, the old Philips having finally been given away. The summer would present the choice of two late-night options: *V* (shape-shifting aliens) on ITV or the Los Angeles games on BBC1. I watched each of them with the sound turned down for fear of waking my parents in their rooms below.

We lived in West London, less than half a mile from Stamford Bridge. Coe had been born a few miles further West in Chiswick, and he (like several of my school contemporaries but unlike me) supported Chelsea Football Club.

When Coe was still young, his family moved from London to Stratford upon Avon. They lived on the edge of town and he would regularly run two miles or so into town and back again on errands for his mother, never using a bicycle, always preferring the feeling of running. Ovett tells a similar story save that in his account the errands were for his father and meant purchasing fags or cans from the corner store. Mick Ovett would even pretend to time the youthful athlete, counting out loud "three, four, five" as he left the house, and starting afresh "twenty-three, twenty-four" as he heard the sounds of his son returning home.

Ovett's mother owned and ran a café; Mrs Coe was an actress who wound down her own career to raise a family. Coe's twin sister was a ballet dancer in her teens, and it is said that she shared his ability to walk or run as if on air.

Coe's mother told the documentary that her son was a nervous child and he flourished only in the absence of competition. Elsewhere, it is recorded that Coe finished disappointingly in his first two efforts at the England Schools championships.

In Sheffield, the Coes lived in Hallamshire, surrounded by doctors and university lecturers. The young Seb Coe was asthmatic and suffered from eczema and hay fever. Unlike Ovett, he failed his 11-plus. This would barely have caused any sort of stir in the Ovett household, but in the Coe family it was seen as a shameful episode, a defeat likely to bring down the status of the whole family. Peter Coe told the future athlete he could either accept then and there he was a failure, as the examination had suggested, or he could work to prove the test wrong. In his mother's words, "He didn't achieve very much. He achieved when it didn't matter, but when it came to the tests, like the 11-plus, nerves got to him so much." Her accent, like her husband's or indeed her son's, shows few signs of any Sheffield influence.

The father's desire for the family to retain its middle class status chimed with the son's need to retain his father's love. He worked harder than he might previously have thought possible. In his studies, and in his running, he was transformed.

"All the top performances come", Peter Coe said, "when it's hurting."

Coe addressed his father by his first name. In his book *The*

Winning Mind he refers at several points to the views of his "coach". A different parent might have allowed his son to address him directly as "father". "I drove us both hard", Peter Coe said, "patience was not my virtue. I expected him to be ready on the dot for training! But he was a splendid fellow, he knew better how to live with me than anyone in the family. He learned obedience, yet by the time he grew up his father wasn't God, he knew that I had feet of clay. We worked on the programme and he never badgered me or questioned the programme." Over the next two years, Coe would shed his early physical weakness and develop into a decent schoolboy athlete.

When Coe was barely 13 his father drew up a projection of progress up to the 1980 Olympics with an optimum 1,500 metres time of 3.30, three minutes faster than the then world record.

The documentary showed a black and white photograph of Coe grimacing with every muscle in his neck tight, as at Moscow. He was then aged just 11 or 12.

In the build up to Moscow, the papers would sell Coe to the British public as "the toff" in contrast to Ovett, "the monster". As a student, Coe talked up aspects of his life which seemed to emphasise his middle-class character, such as his admiration of the American novelists Steinbeck, Hemmingway and Bellow, his love of jazz, and his desire to follow his father by working in industry. Part of this involved an early espousal of the politics that Mrs Thatcher was still cautious about testing on the country. As Coe told one interviewer:

"I'm a great believer in personal liberty, and I do believe in the interplay of market forces. If anybody is good enough and in demand whatever field they are in, then you will find people are prepared to pay. And if somebody can make a living out of what they are good at, I don't really see what grounds anybody can say no."

After his gold at the 1980 Olympics, Coe spent many hours

negotiating the first advertising contract for an amateur athlete, for which special dispensation was required from the running authorities. He earned a footballer's salary in becoming the public face of Instant Horlicks.

When Coe won gold over 1500 metres in the 1980 Olympics, his success and above all his victory over his compatriot Ovett was portrayed as a great triumph of the English middle classes. In the words of the *Daily Mail*, "He lifted the soul, he ennobled his art, he dignified his country." The papers were surely right to emphasise their rivalry; Coe and Ovett did represent two opposed strategies for life.

Something more was at stake however than just the surface distinction between the market trader's boy and the manager's son. For as Ovett said repeatedly, in terms of background there was more that they had in common than separated them. The early lives of each were dominated by a single strong parent. Both came originally from Southern England, Coe, the younger athlete, was just twelve months younger than Ovett. Both were students, even if the media insisted on taking Coe's Sport Science more seriously than Ovett's Art. Most people in Britain were waged employees, each of Peter Coe and Mick Ovett were set apart (if, admittedly, in subtly different ways) from the working-class majority.

As well as class, the runners differed in their approach on the track and beyond.

When they ran, Ovett was generally seen as a "kicker" who relied on his finishing pace, while Coe was a "bunny", who depended on a very fast first half of the race to wear his opponents into submission. But neither style was innate, Coe's self-invention between 1976 and 1978 as a front-runner came about for specific reasons.

As a schoolboy athlete, Coe was seen as a 1500 and 3000 metre runner. The assumption is that, as an athlete ages, he or she loses the ability to run quickly over very short distances and will gravitate towards longer distances. Ovett's fastest time over 5000 metres was achieved 12 years after his best over 400 metres. Coe turned to the 800 metres late, in 1976, with his father's blessing, after he reduced his best 800 metre time by three seconds in a single race. It became clear, without anyone planning it, that the distance suited him perfectly.

Coe's difficulty on choosing the shorter distance is that while it suited him well, British athletics already supplied a world-class rival, Ovett. Moreover this rival appeared to possess an unparalleled asset, his finish. Coe became a front-runner, in short, to counter his rival's best weapon.

Coe's adopted tactic of running a first lap of the 800 metres in under 50 seconds brought him both success and failure. It was the key to his first world record, over 800 metres at Oslo in July 1979, during which Coe's 200-metre splits were timed as 24.0, 26.0, 24.8 and 27.0. The extraordinary period of the race was the third 200 metres, during which Coe powered away from a field which including Mike Boit, by now a World Cup silver medallist. The Oslo time was in turn the key to Coe's two further world records in the next six weeks, over the mile and the 1500 metres.

The front-runner's mantle however brought defeat in competition over 800 metres in the 1978 European Championships, and at the Olympics two years later. Determined not to repeat his bronze from Prague, Coe knew not to run a first lap in less than 50 seconds. Having worked out how not to run, he forgot the simpler task of how best to race. He ran passively in the 800 metres at Moscow, leaving the way to Ovett to claim the Olympic gold.

For far too long, in short, Coe was running negatively, against Ovett.

Defeat

Through my fourth year of school athletics, my body was intermittently fixed and broken. I also had to face competition, finally, from a runner of my own standard. Pete was in his final year. He had been a cricketer but, after winning in the spring athletic championships, joined the athletics team. He was a year older than me, and at his best a second faster than me over 800 metres. I would meet him by chance in London two years later, by which time he was running in the national squad.

Pete secured one victory over me which irked. Declining to recognise my new school record in the under-17 800 metres, Charlie told me that he would recognise it so long as I could match the time in a time trial on the track (it was now of course a year later). Pete agreed to pace me, and we completed the first 400 metres in just under 60 seconds. The second lap we finished in 61 seconds.

I narrowed on Pete in the last straight but he finished a metre in front of me. Neither of us had broken the 2 minute barrier, which I had crossed a year earlier.

I was also watching two younger athletes. James was the fastest 800 metre runner in the year below. His father was a well-known politician, avaricious and flamboyantly crooked. At school, James struggled to escape from the shadow of his father's reputation. On the track, he seemed a little light, good over 1500 metres but without a strong finishing kick. Later, I would regret having underestimated his ability.

Alexis was two years younger than James, he had a heavier build and a faster kick. I watched him through the summer nibbling away at my under-15 800 metres record. Four or five times he came within a second of beating it, but never quite had the competition to take him through the remaining fractions of a second.

At the end of the year, Charlie had the pick of two school athletics captains, and he followed his convention of choosing one track runner and one field athlete. For some time I had assumed that I would be the track captain in my final year. Instead, he chose Kris, our best runner over 400 metres. In a childlike fit of pique, of which I am not proud, I responded by resigning from the team.

By the age of eighteen, I had suffered repeated minor tears of my left achilles tendon. Runner's guides distinguish between tendonitis, a condition where the tendon thickens but the thickening dissipates after a period of rest, and tendinosis, which is when the tendon suffers chronic, microscopic tears, a condition for which the ultimate cure is surgery. I had first been injured at the age of fourteen. Never since had I enjoyed a full running season without even minor injury. My injuries had long since passed from the occasional to the chronic.

The range of my injuries, moreover, seemed to be spreading. I had already suffered one bout of exercise-related asthma, and for the next two years was prone to chest infections. My knees were often sore. There seemed to be some relationship between the recurring weakness in my left tendon and pains in my right knee. Had I wanted to continue, I should have asked to see a consultant specialising in sports injuries. I did not ask, Charlie did not think to look for one.

Most of my penultimate running year at school was lost to an achilles tendon tear. My running future offered no prospect other than further injury.

I had met a tall, beautiful woman who encouraged me to run but did not run herself. We drove to cross country races; she cheered me on from beside the school athletics track. For a year we were as inseparable as the school discipline allowed. Still caught in a fixed routine which I could bend but not break altogether, we wrote at evenings, overwhelmed by the self-consciousness of our love. Her letters were shape-poetry, tears of absence giving way to joyful laughter.

Breaking out of the institution after our night-time roll-call, she would drive me to distant clubs and bars where we danced. We walked at night in view of the river where once my father had rowed. We hid, alone, invisible in summer fields.

When eventually our relationship cooled, some of what I had loved about running was taken away. For months, we continued to meet, but our reconciliations were painful and incomplete. And then, finally, all had ended. I wanted to wallow in the misery of the loss of a relationship that I had thought would last for ever. I wanted to stay inside. I desired the sorrow of my own company. I did not want to run.

Unwilling to train on the track and more or less unable as a result of injury, I settled instead for following Joe's prescription: more and more miles, especially through autumn and winter. Returning to my house afterwards, in my room alone, I built a box of words for my anguish, filling page upon page with stories of people lost in a city where chance encounters never happened, where relationships crumbled, where strangers passed unknowingly at night. At another age, running had saved me from the introversion of adolescence. Now, the self-pity overcame my defences.

I had stopped running for the school. The other pupils were arrogant and rich. I did not identify with the institution; I hated the unfreedom and privilege that it represented. But by ceasing to run on its behalf, I deprived myself of the opportunity for competition. I enjoyed the company of Joe's young charges, and when I could run with them I did. But summer was coming, my last year at school. When it was over, I would move, returning to London.

I did not stir myself to race competitively with Joe's group; I could have had no more than a single summer running with them.

My left achilles was still sore, I had damaged my tibialis anterior, the muscle at the front of my right leg that pulls the foot up. I ran twelve miles along roads with a friend, Jim. On my return, the arch of my foot hurt. I convinced myself that it was collapsing. I bought sprays to keep my legs warm, I read in magazines about the utility of an ice bath after running. I did not know whether to walk in an exercise bandage or not. Most frustratingly, none of the other runners I knew, Paul, Luke or anyone else, ever seemed to be injured. What, I asked myself, was I doing wrong?

There is something particularly debilitating about running injured. The problem may not be so serious that you cannot run at all. But you are conscious of it. You know that if you really relax properly and run full out, the result will in all likelihood be further pain. You conserve your energy, you shift your weight around, you hold your body back.

It may be that nobody watching would know that you were injured. But if you know your body, you know that you are running wrong.

I understand now that I was winding down, but had someone said that to me at the time I would have protested. I believed I had every desire to continue. I ran in the autumn and the summer. I continued to enter the various school competitions, the cross-country and the athletics final. I continued to run with Joe's group, and at my aunts, and back home. When I ran, I was just as determined to finish first as I had ever been. When I trained, I was still in practice for competition. Friends smuggled small quantities of marijuana into the school (the younger boys smoked more easily obtained dried bananas). To protect my runners' lungs, I refused to inhale but settled for varieties of cake, cookies, even specially-planned ice cream.

There were athletics clubs at my university, I never ran there. In my three years as a student the closest I came was a couple of miles jogging once around the football fields with a rower friend. I did not run, I had ceased to enjoy the sport.

Others continued running without a break, including Pete and Tom. Others only took up running again a decade later, as I did.

How good could I have been? One evening, my father encouraged me to put less effort into my running and to concentrate on my schoolwork. "You do know", he said, "that you are better at schoolwork than you are at running?" I protested, there were plenty of my pupils who were my superior at languages or maths. I had never met the runner who could match me over 1500 metres.

When I look back at the times I ran they show to me two possible trajectories. I was a year behind the runners generally considered late developers. Had I continued and been consistently lucky I might have become the sort of athlete you see losing out at the first rounds of major games. Or, more likely, I might have got stuck at a point little further from the one I reached. I would have run until a further injury hit me, more debilitating than the ones which brought my running to an end.

My father brought me back from these imagined revelries. He described to me how happy he was to have quit rowing when he did. "If I hadn't", he warned me, "I would never have passed my degree."

My final year of running I began training with Joe, jogging in a large group along the three-mile-long straight lines of our nearest park. The autumn cross-country, as ever, was a disappointment. I remained with Paul for the first two miles, but he kicked on and I tired, my feet heavy on the damp ground.

Paul had chosen to specialise in two events normally kept

separate, the 110m hurdles, and the 3000m steeplechase. The latter ended in another defeat, as I never worked out a proper plan to win. Paul wore me out by taking an early lead. I held back, confident in my finish. He gained two clear metres over me by accelerating out of the last water jump, and I stumbled over the final hurdle, when I should have ducked just above it. Afterwards, we found ways of avoiding each other in competition. Paul left me alone in the 800m and 1500m, races I expected to win. I avoided the steeplechase, knowing I could not catch him.

Yet as I approached my last 800m and 1500m finals, in Paul's absence, and short of serious injury, I did not believe that I had a rival capable of beating me.

My heat of the 800 metres was a slow race. I was racing boys in my own year and the year below. The former I had beaten repeatedly over the past five years. Most of the latter would have raced me two years before, when we had last been in the same age category. None had come close to me then, or should have now. From the outset, I charged straight to the front. Then, I slowed almost immediately, holding the entire group in a great crowd behind me. We reached the 200 metre mark in forty five seconds, fully double the pace I could manage at full sprint. No one overtook.

At one lap, the time was eighty seconds, still slow, but enough to have begun to stretch the field a little. Stage by stage, I increased the pace thereafter: running successive hundred metres in 16, 15, 14 and 13 seconds. The overall time was very slow, at around two minutes twenty seconds. I felt relaxed. I had won and I was not injured. I felt wholly in control of those all about me.

The other heat, if I had had the guile to notice, was ten seconds faster.

There were various people watching the 800 metres final. They included my house master, who I disliked ever since he had replaced his much loved and exuberantly camp predecessor. There were other boys there too, conscripts from the junior years of the house, who had been encouraged to attend by boys in my year. My father was there too, speaking I suppose to one of his former contemporaries whose children were now at the school.

The starter's gun went. I left the start cold, as I often did. Within a few paces though, I had pushed my way to the front. I ran with my chest straight and my arms working to my side. I was a strong runner. I grimaced at those around me and as I stared they parted. I retained my aura of invincibility.

I had enjoyed the 800 metre heat, now I attempted the same tactics in the final. We reached the 200-metre mark in around forty seconds. No one overtook me. I stretched, at one lap, the time was 71 or 72 seconds, but a couple of boys remained with me. There was just a lap to go. My body felt comfortable, my brain clear.

Sensibly, I thought, I had saved energy for my second final (the 1500m) later in the day. I felt invincible. The thought did not occur to me that by setting off at a gentle pace, I had failed to run the legs off the one or two of my challengers who had ever run at all close to me. I had converted a two lap race into a one lap sprint. This suited them far better than it suited me. At this distance, I heard no shouts, no applause. I could not even hear the sounds of the two runners just behind me.

I increased my speed at each 100 metre interval, building towards a sprinter's pace. At the final bend, James suddenly darted in front of me. The move caught me cold, he had never beaten me, he had never come close to beating me.

At the start of the last straight he was two metres ahead. I tried to increase my pace. I lengthened my stride, I lowered my head.

I tried to force my body to relax. I trusted myself to go faster and did go faster but not fast enough. James won by half a second.

Love, Spiritual Or Otherwise

"We can have no knowledge of Love", my father recorded in his diary, "apart from our experience of love. We cannot imagine a universal, we cannot imagine God's love for us, if we have no experience of love – if we have not loved others ourselves for only loving gives experience of love, being loved does not." In his new-found philosophy the loneliness of consciousness was to be filled by the love of God or the love of fellow humanity, and all the other ways of filling the gap were bound to fail. "In order to help the simple", he wrote, "the church makes the good life consist in the performance of ceremonies and rituals. The intelligent, seeing that these are not God spurn the church, and those that are foolish turn to other things and are unhappy whilst the wise use the ceremonies to help their understanding."

"It is a pity that I did not start writing these thoughts until I had already started to shed my scepticism," the diary continued, "though of course the process of shedding is by no means certain to continue in a straight line progression."

The shedding would continue, but progress remained far from straight.

A photograph kept by my grandmother shows my father "the Oxford rowing Blue and sculler adjust[ing] the bowler hat on Miss Jean Macdonald". It was election night. Although there continue to be sporadic references to rowing throughout my father's diary, from this point onwards its central concern is my father's search for a lover who would share his growing enthusiasm for the Roman Catholic faith.

My father was in the process of resiling from Anglicanism for the very reason that the older religion seemed to require a deeper and more taxing faith. Yet this process proved harder than he liked. One difficulty was that Catholicism had if anything an even stronger commitment to the postwar orthodoxy of no sex before marriage.

"One must have the tangible", my father wrote down, "the touchable, aethereal satisfaction is no good, so unexciting. One must be excited. This is falling, I suppose. Well I have fallen. Right off that pinnacle. All that I work for now is "beds" instead of heaven ... Now when I meet a woman there is only one object, perhaps this way perhaps that. Then how can I become a Catholic. Yet I must. Why can one never have both?"

"Faith in goodness is a loveable quality", my father's diary recorded, "and it is a fact that wherever I see, anything that I call good, anyone that I admire or want to be like, anything that I would wish myself to do then these things can only be reached through Christianity."

Yet he could see another view, "the devil trots out the familiar jargon: 'you are such a person that, being conditioned by your Christian environment and race heredity, you have Christian ethical standards, feeling emotions such as remorse when you break them and moral satisfaction when you keep to them. Besides, man is psychologically so constituted that he is happier when he can throw himself whole-heartedly into some religion. Communists and Roman Catholics, commissars and saints are filled with a sense of purpose & fulfilment & so of unity and harmony. The more persuasive the doctrine the more convincing it is, the more one is at peace with oneself because there is less threat to one's harmony.'"

"'But do not imagine that this proves the existence of a single objective ethic. In fact it is obvious that this satisfaction is derived from differing even contradictory things by different people.'"

Love itself proved very different from my father's Platonic imaginings. His diary records eyes, legs, mouths, skin, hair that is only half curled, women clad in quiet colours and a few jewels. One vision in particular was careless, lazy, nervous, trembling, dreamy, soft to touch. "She is not put out by the events of the world whatever they may be, because she is only half aware of them. She is shy and yet does not bother to conquer the world and so her shyness."

"There is never any need to explain to her", my father writes, "She has a great capacity to arouse affection and love (all those around her obey this). She loves others and others love her. Though whether she loves them and they love her as a dream I don't know. So she is good not because of ethics, but in the way that beauty is good. This combined with the acuteness of mind and with the understanding is irresistible. She is pure; her purity is greater because it does not depend on rules."

"One wishes that one could make oneself one of the characters in her dreams and stay there and be nothing else for ever."

My father could only explain how he felt through metaphor: "A man once fell in love with pictures; and since he was very rich, he would set out to buy the most beautiful pictures in the world. For twenty years he travelled everywhere, looked at everything, and by then he knew which were the most beautiful pictures in the world ... He bought them all, for he was very rich."

"He took them into a private room where no-one else could see them, and he locked the room ... They were with the room the whole time but with him only some of the time. So he shut himself up in the room and stayed there for days. But they still weren't his. So he took them all off the walls and placed them all around him. He lay on the floor and pulled them over him till they pressed right down on top of him."

"Then he threw them off and lit a fire and burnt them one by one till there were none left. Then he realised that they still weren't his and that the fire had gone out so he could not even throw himself into it."

My father sculled at Oxford in the summer, after defeat in the boat race, winning both the University's single sculls and the pairs. Victory in the double sculls was especially pleasing as a key rival was the Oxford President and his school contemporary, Christopher Davidge. The river is narrow at Oxford and the boat club had constructed a special semaphore system so that the racers could know whether they were ahead or behind on the clock. "At the first semaphore", my father recalls, "we were behind, but at the second, we were in front. It was only after the race that I learned that Davidge and his crew member had rowed into the river bank."

In the single sculls, my father also beat Tony Fox, who would later represent Britain in the 1952 Helsinki Olympics (where Fox came fourth in the single sculls, the best performance by a British sculler from 1924 to the present day) and at the 1956 Olympics in Melbourne.

My father prepared for that year's Henley regatta by rowing the twenty miles from Oxford to Henley. After the regatta had finished, he rowed his boat the remaining 40 miles from Henley to his home in London.

After Rivalry

As a boy, Coe was sent away for a weekend to train with David Hemery, the Olympic gold medallist in the 110 metres hurdles. Much of the talk was given over to the joys of athletics and the potential for each runner to realise his or her ambitions. Then Hemery paused. With emphasis, he said, "You're all going to get injuries, and the true worth of an athlete will always come to the fore when he is injured."

Both athletes spent large periods of the years from 1981 to 1984 out of action. Ovett's difficulties began after the knee injury he suffered in December 1981. Over the next two-and-a-half years his further injuries included a hamstring tear, a knee injury at the start of 1983, and a leg muscle pull in the build up to the 1983 World Championships. In 1984, he nearly drowned on Bondi beach, after which he caught bronchitis which remained with him until the 1984 Olympics.

Coe, for his part, had been suffering from a serious blood infection, probably since late 1982. Ill, in summer 1983, he lost in a minor 1500 metres bringing to the end a run of 36 successive victories over that distance.

Both were struggling to qualify for the 1984 Olympics, their places were under challenge from younger British athletes including Steve Cram, who as a 20-year-old had come eighth in the 1500 metres at Moscow before winning the World Championship over the same distance in 1983. Four years younger than Coe, he was approaching his best years. Also in the mix was Peter Elliot from Rotherham who had been for several years a decent 800-metre runner. He had recently shifted to 1500 metres, knocking ten seconds off his best in beating Cram in early 1984.

Four athletes were battling for three places, and when Elliott sprinted past Coe at that year's Southern Countries, on the morning of the selection meeting prior to the 1984 Olympics, Coe's congratulation of Elliott suggested that he saw that his own last chance had gone. The selectors duly chose Elliott and even publicised their decision, before panicking at the prospect of a Coe press campaign, and reinstating him for both the 800 and 1500 metres alongside Ovett.

Ovett would go and I was content. Ovett for his part was outraged that the selectors had originally ignored Coe in favour of Elliot, a novice over 1500 metres.

Ovett did just enough to reach the final. His chest infection was aggravated by conditions in Los Angeles, including smog and day-time temperatures of up to 102 degrees. After his first heat in the 800 metres, his hands were limp, his breathing shallow and he felt light-headed. He had the misfortune to draw Joachim Cruz of Brazil in both the heats and the semi-finals, each of which Cruz then won in brilliantly fast times. Ovett somehow made it to the final, relying on sheer force of character to qualify, throwing himself at the line, making it through in the last place. It was obvious to everyone watching that he was exhausted, but his fatigue was far from surprising. Ovett's time in qualifying from the semi-final (1.44.81) was a whole second faster than his winning time in the Olympic final of four years before.

Ovett did run, finished last, and was taken to hospital to recover. His wife Rachel was terrified that he might be suffering a heart attack. The British team manager tried everything to persuade him to withdraw from the 1500 metres heats.

Coe came second to Cruz, who remained exactly three metres ahead of the British athlete throughout.

After such a collapse, Ovett should barely have been capable of running again. But he did run three days later, winning his 1500 metre qualifying heat, if in a slow time. He was then fourth in the semi-final, after which he experienced the same pains as he had at the equivalent stage of the 800 metres. Rachel spent the last evening trying once again to persuade her husband not to run again. Coe and Cram, for their part, seemed to be in much better condition: Cram winning his semi-final, Coe qualifying from his with energy to spare.

With one lap of the final to go, Coe looked backwards over his right shoulder. He was second, behind him were Cram and then Ovett. Coe's finish was faster than Cram's. The only question was whether Ovett might yet force himself into contention. But the older runner was struggling to breathe, made himself to the inside, and dropped out, with just 400 metres to go.

Coe gathered himself and sprinted for gold. At home, watching the race, I mourned the passing of Ovett's moment. "I take pride", Ovett wrote afterwards, "in being part of one of the greatest 1500 metre races ever run."

I remember little of Coe's victory. I recall rather an image of Ovett, doubled over, his knees bent and his face hidden from the camera. He was balding by now and he looked old. The camera returned to the race. Next, the event finished, there was a second shot of Ovett. By now he was looking straight towards the camera. A medic was passing a white towel across his face. His jaw was set and he seemed to be on the verge of tears. There were interviews with Coe and Cram, after which I remember a further image of Ovett being strapped into a stretcher. "Poor Steve Ovett", David Coleman said, "we'll get news of him as soon as possible." Then, he and Brendan Foster went through the images of the finish one further time, "All I'd like to see", Coleman said, "is Ovett fit and well and in action again."

His friends had not wanted Ovett to race; they were convinced that he might yet do his body lasting damage. He insisted on running, he tried everything. He showed his determination even when his body had nothing left to give.

There could be dignity, I learned, even in defeat.

What does it matter when an athlete loses? Does a defeat cancel out all the good that has gone before? For what, anyway, does victory count? Pete's Coe answer was that his son had to keep on running, for ever, because his love was conditional and at the moment of defeat that love could be taken away from him. That answer was good enough for him, in order to motivate his son, and in life fear is often a sufficient motive. But Ovett was running differently: in hope, freely and from a genuine love of the sport.

His memoir attests to the anti-climax that Ovett felt after having defeated the world in the 800 metres at Moscow. "Elation gradually filtered through, but it took a time … I did not expect to win the 800 metres so easily and I think the race lost some of its intrigue by the simplicity of my victory."

He has spoken in interviews since of the unsatisfactory nature of his triumph, "I had won everything that I wanted to win up to the Olympics, and I wanted to win the Olympics, I won the Olympics, and I thought 'There should be more than this'."

When I play over in my head the images of the Moscow 1500 metres final, I ask why Ovett never kicked. There were at least three moments at which it would have been surely easier to go than to have done what Ovett actually did and stay. At 250 metres from the finish, at 120 metres and at 90 metres: each time his stride began to lengthen before he paused. Each time, he returned to the inside.

Perhaps he had made his point, he was the 800-metre champion. His success was already total. If he had stirred himself to victory, what would that have proved? Was his victory conditional, was he expected to race and win, in the next Olympics, and four years after that? How many more times would he have to triumph, to earn peace? What final victory could there ever be?

If I am right, and in some way Ovett was content with defeat, he should not be criticised. The neoliberal vision – a permanent revolution of endless competition – is a utopia so dark and so destructive of those signed up to it, that not one person in a million would choose to live consistently by its rules.

When Coe tells his life story, he makes much of Ovett's supposed fear of him. "I first realised", he has written, "that from Steve's point of view I was more than just a rival at the end of the 1977 season, which was my first major outdoor season. Little comments had come my way. For instance, when asked what he thought of my prospects, he thought I would never be fast enough to run a really world class 800 metres. It was only after that remark that I broke Andy Carter's UK record."

Elsewhere, Coe said, "I always had the feeling that when the gap began to disappear ... the rivalry would become greater, and with it his need to prove himself."

Ovett's career, when both he and Coe were fit, was Coe's equal. Coe's superiority was in posting record times. Here too Coe wanted to portray their eventual convergence as evidence of his superiority: "Steve had said so often ... that all he cared about was winning races ... Yet by August [1979] he had a carefully orchestrated record-breaking circus on the road with the help of Andy Norman. It seemed that my records forced him to break cover."

Similar dynamics can be seen in the Moscow Olympics, Coe blaming his defeat in the 800 metres on his own failings, "I'd grown accustomed to taking liberties in one or two races in the previous year, to running wide from the back, and now, in the most devastating way, I'd discovered you can't do that in an Olympic final."

Coe did not acknowledge that Ovett had run well. Far from it, he suggested that Ovett's victory could be put down to the hard physical manner in which his rival had forced himself from the back of the field. "Only after I'd seen the video did I realise how physical Steve had been. I felt it had contributed to the tattiness of the race. It lowered the standing of athletics. I was very surprised the East Germans and the French didn't make more of it." Coe was the moral victor in the race, it followed, Ovett only won because he had cheated.

Ovett's response to Coe's victory in the 1500 metres was rather more generous, "I ran the best race I could but was beaten by two better guys." His vision of life was broad enough to acknowledge another runner's talent.

Through their careers Coe and Ovett experienced triumph and disaster differently. Ovett fought hard, but once the race had ended nothing seemed more natural to him than to congratulate his rivals, still more so if they had beaten him with aplomb. He was delighted to recognise another runner achieving something extraordinary. Ovett had no ambitions in the sport beyond running itself. In an interview three months before the Moscow Olympics, he told Athletics Weekly that "some people have very definite ambitions in life – they want a house, marriage, a fridge ... But I'm just meandering through and enjoying what I can."

Ovett says that in the aftermath of Coe's defining victory, the 1500 metres at Moscow, his rival could not relax. "Where did you finish?" Coe asked him. Only with Ovett's answer, that he had come a mere third was Coe satisfied. Yet on the occasions when both athletes lost, Ovett could be seen comforting the younger man. So it was in Prague in 1978. There was even something of the same attempt at solidarity at the awards ceremony after the Moscow 800 metres.

It was that capacity for warmth, sympathy and human solidarity which represented for me Ovett's victory.

Triumph

The 800 metre final, my penultimate school race, had finished before lunch, and I had two clear hours before my last race, the 1500 metre final. My father and I drove off to eat. We talked about those who were absent, my grandmother who had died earlier that same year, my half-sisters who were working in London, and my mother who was also away. We discussed his own memories of the long years in which he had been a successful rower. My father told me, not for the first time, that when he had run at school he had best enjoyed middle distance races.

The time passed slowly; there was one obvious topic which we could not broach. I was a relaxed runner. Between my fourth and fifth gears, the shape of my body did not alter. I did not lift my arms higher, my face would not redden. I did not give the impression of trying, even when I was hurting inside. I had just been defeated by a runner a whole year younger than myself. I was burning with shame but on the track I must have appeared to him almost passive.

Why had I not fought harder?

I came back from lunch for the 1500-metre final, walking away from the other competitors to prepare myself. I warmed up with a couple of gentle laps, jogging at a pace so slow that I was barely walking. The third lap, I did not even run but simply walked. Returning to the track, I saw Alexis, who was preparing for finals of his own. Alongside me, he had run once or twice with Joe's group. He too had begun to shed the cocoon of school. We both wished each other well.

I saw Luke, my contemporary. We had run together, intermittently, through the past five years. He had grown to become a fast runner over 1500 metres and over longer distances. The race was his last school final, just as it was my own. For two of those years, we had also been in a band together. I was the bassist, Luke the drummer. We had also been in the audience together at several gigs. Luke liked James as little as I did. He knew that I was hurting.

I prepared by breathing slowly, deep through my nose into my hearts and lungs. I concentrated as keenly as I could.

We assembled for the start. When I had run the 800-metres final earlier that day, I had run without any consciousness of the possibility of defeat. My innocence was now gone. I had no sense of whether James could sustain a second fast race in one day, indeed, looking at him as we lined up, he seemed to be still tired from the morning. But this race was not one that I would risk by taking lightly. If not James, anyone else, perhaps Luke could beat me.

On the bell, I made straight for the front. At each 100 metres I picked up my knees and intensified my pace. I ran the first lap in well under 50 seconds, a time little different from my fastest 800 metre pace. Looking over my shoulder, I could see that the closest runners were already 50 metres behind me. The boys at the end of the field were a further 50 metres behind the main chasing pack.

The school's headmaster turned to his companion, "of course, there's no way that Renton will stick to the end". I did not lack motivation. If I had, those words would have supplied all that I needed.

At my peak as an athlete, I enjoyed best the feeling of my heart, lungs and legs working together without difficulty. Whatever tasks I had in life, their need would cease to press. My concentration would turn inwards. Even my eyes' focus would shorten. There were other people around me, both on the track, and around it. My father was watching from somewhere on the finishing stretch. All of them vanished. All my brain could register was the simple repetition of one foot landing after another. All I knew was whether my legs ached, and how they ached, and whether the ache was so urgent that it would impact on my time. All I cared about was whether my arms were at the right height, and if I was punching too high or too low.

My legs were not hurting. My lower left leg in particular did not feel sore. My lungs seemed clear enough and my chest and arms were relaxed. A thought did cross my mind, I hoped that Luke was holding out against James.

At the end of the next lap, utterly calm, I felt no need to turn and see whether anyone was closing on me.

The third lap was lonely. My best times at any distance have only ever come when I was surrounded by athletes running at my own speed. To pace a 1500-metre race properly you have to fight constantly the natural temptation to run a bend or a straight just a second or two slow. The runner's risk is that he deceives himself. As your legs begin to ache, it is easy to pretend that a slow period can be made up later. You let the pace drop, and a fast time turns to something less.

At the bell, my time was three minutes dead. All that motivated me now was the thought of breaking the school record. To match that, I would have to run the last lap in well under a minute.

With 400 metres to go, and no other athlete within 50 metres of me, I began to sprint. It was my second hard race of the day. I did not know if I would ever run again. I had built up a bank of miles through the winter. Now was my chance to really press. I ran into the bends. I held my head poised, forwards and low.

I finished the race in 4 minutes and three seconds. I was a second or two outside the school record. I waited and watched as the other runners approached, from 100 metres, then 50 metres away. Soon, they too were finished. I saw Luke and together we ran a last 400 metre victory lap. I was proud of my race. As a spectator, I had rarely seen such a one-sided race. It was the moment I retired. I have never run since, to any proper standard.

Later that day, the prizes were awarded, and a reluctant school headmaster handed me the 1500-metre trophy, an eighteen-inch monster of a silver cup with shields around a wooden base recording the previous years' winners. The other prize-winners were all dressed neatly in the school athletics team's maroon colours. I by contrast was wearing my own white vest. I felt that I had triumphed not just against twelve other boys but against the school itself. The cup would be passed over in due course to another disliked teacher, my housemaster. It would then feature, centre stage, in our end of year photographs.

My father finally asked me, "why didn't you run like that earlier?"

Conversion

As my father prepared for the next boat race, there was every reason for optimism. He was at his peak as an athlete; there were few rowers in Britain his equal. He had shown in the previous year's sculls that he was a prodigious talent. After five straight defeats, the Oxford crew was desperate for revenge. Davidge, the previous year's absentee, returned once more as President and stroke.

My father was 'still short and stiff', one journalist wrote, 'but he has a much truer drive from the stretcher than last year and rows a more consistent blade.' The only other member of the previous year's Oxford crew to compete again was P. Gladstone, a descendant of the Victorian politician, and a veteran of National Service with the Palestine Police.

As the crews approached the stake boats, they hit a brief squall. The water was now very rough, and both boats found themselves low, having taken on water. Oxford had chosen the Surrey station. The race began. After less than a minute, more water started coming over the sides of the Oxford boat. For about twenty strokes the crew tried to keep going. They were working hard simply to stay afloat.

On the BBC launch were John Snagge and the former Oxford and Cambridge blues Jock Clapperton and Ronnie Symonds. It was Clapperton who described the start: "There is no doubt about it, Cambridge did go away beautifully in the very, very rough water … They are nearly four lengths ahead … I have never seen in many, many Boat Races a crew go away as quickly as Cambridge have. Oxford have in their start made very, very heavy weather of it, much more so than Cambridge. They seem to be rowing at a much lower rating and incapable of getting it up. It also looks uncomfortable, they are not together and it looks to me as though they are shipping an enormous amount of water. It will surprise me if they are able to keep going at this rate much longer."

Snagge cut in, "Yes, Oxford are shipping so much water that I doubt if they are going to last at all."

Then Symonds, "Well Cambridge are right away out there in the distance. They have made, as you heard, a beautiful start. It was watermanship. At the moment we are almost level with Oxford's stem and Oxford are sinking"

Snagge went on, "Yes, I am afraid Oxford are sinking, they have stopped rowing in point of fact. They have got waterlogged and are sinking. Just let me tell you that Cambridge on their side have cut right across and the Cambridge cox looks round for a moment to see what is happening, but he seems also in trouble. Oxford have stopped rowing and they are waterlogged, they have stopped and they have only got as far as just to the corner of Beverley Brook and have actually ceased to row. Cambridge have come right across the river and are trying to come across to the shelter, and of course the rule is that if they can finish the course and don't get into more serious trouble, they are indeed the winners. It is for the umpire to decide."

"The umpire is past the Oxford boat and has left them behind, waterlogged, where they are being picked up by other boats, they are afloat but waterlogged, that is to say, they are going to be picked up in a moment or two."

Cambridge by now were rowing beside the Surrey bank, with every intention of finishing the course and winning.

At this point, the umpire had an important decision to make. An agreement between the two universities held that if at the start of the race either boat suffered a serious accident, and in the view of the umpire the accident was not the fault of any individual in the crew, the umpire had the power to recall and restart the crews. In practice, a recall was impossible. The boats were supported by a multitude of following craft, whose wash made the water conditions impossible for racing, and in any event, too much time had been wasted, the ideal tide for racing had already been lost. So, rather than restart, the real decision was whether to race again, on a new day.

Oxford could blame the conditions, which were undoubtedly blustery. Snagge, in his own commentary, complained that even the BBC launch was taking on water. Cambridge however had a perfectly good answer, if the conditions were so bad, and Oxford had done nothing wrong, why was it that only they and not Cambridge sank?

The umpire was the Reverend G. A. Ellison, the Bishop of Willesden. He decided to order a re-race, which was organised for the following Monday.

In the build up to the re-race, the feeling of most observers was that Cambridge would win. Oxford were said to be damaged psychologically by the experience of sinking, and by having to put their fate in the hands of the umpire. So it proved. Cambridge raced to an early lead. By Hammersmith Bridge, they were twelve seconds ahead. Cambridge's winning time was 20 minutes 15 seconds, a dead heat with their winning time of the year before. Their winning margin was 12 lengths, making this the most one-sided boat race in five decades,

There was a particular edge to that year's boat race. The winners of the race had been invited in advance to the United States where they were to race against Yale and Harvard. Cambridge's subsequent victories in that competition were widely reported and the triumphant college oarsmen were presented to His Majesty King George VI. Later that year, racing on behalf of Britain in the European championships, Cambridge won gold. They were on their way to deserved fame.

Defeat must have been pointed for my father; it was the day after his twenty-first birthday. He did not ask to be considered for the following year's race.

Days after defeat, my father finally converted, "Two days ago I was received into the Catholic church. It was strange that such a 'joyous' moment should in a way be so depressing. The night before I could not do a thing except to wonder whether or not to fall in love with a certain girl and to be preoccupied like that when heaven waited... I spent an hour at Blackfriars just sitting or kneeling. Put one-self into the hands of God and it is all right one need not worry. Perhaps I did succeed in doing that and things became looser. But the next day holding a card and making the vow; this wasn't becoming a Catholic and I was mainly worrying about what other people were thinking anyhow. But the form had to be gone through perhaps I had become a Catholic before."

"Then Communion and the body of God sticking to one's mouth. I was unable to swallow the flesh of our Lord."

"Then all was over and it might as well not have happened. Or might it? The world is the same. I am the same yet I have eaten of the flesh and received the mark."

Learning To Run Again

I have often stopped running. After a sufficient break, I have always gone back to it, hoping to rediscover the energy which I had lost when I stopped.

I started running again in my mid-twenties after an eight-year gap. My partner and I were living with friends in South Liverpool; one of them invited me to join him for his evening run around Sefton Park. I told him a little of my running history before we began. He was six feet two, and had a natural distance runner's lengthy stride. I let him race far into the distance after barely half a mile. When we met up back at the house he told me bluntly, "My God, you're unfit."

Our friend moved to Japan. On his departure, my partner and I rented his house. We remained just a couple of hundred metres from the Park. So my running began again. I recall passing the aviary at the Park's centre. I remember the ground flat, damp and soft, beneath my feet. After a month or two rediscovering how to run, I began to overtake other athletes, them on a gentle mid-morning stroll, me chasing their shadows as fast as I could.

The perimeter of Sefton Park is two-and-a-half miles. A river runs through the park and there is a lake at the South end. Right in the middle of the park is Lark Lane, a district of cafes and bars, a place for people to relax before partying on Saturdays, and an area to which those incapable of sleep would return on Sunday mornings. I soon added a second lap of the park to my starting one.

It was in Liverpool that I finally took up cycling, an exercise I had disdained in my youth, on the grounds that if I could get anywhere just as quickly by running, why require the hassle of a bike that might be stolen? Living in Liverpool I finally worked out that no matter how fast I could run, and I was of course much slower than I had been, a bike was quicker. Returning home from the city centre took me down a steep hill, my hood pulled back above my head as I descended.

It was a hill so steep that I could hardly brake. All I could do was just hope that not one of the cars was intending to turn left.

We were in Liverpool because of work. I had completed a PhD, and was appointed to a two-year university teaching post, covering for a colleague who was on long-term research leave. In my first year, I also volunteered for the role of union branch secretary. I had held lesser union posts before and there seemed to be no other volunteers.

My teaching duties were not onerous, I had sufficient time to continue my research. At university, I had been not merely on the Left, but in particular an anti-racist. My undergraduate dissertation, my PhD, and my first few books were all celebrations of key moments in the history of anti-racist activism.

I was determined to publish, and I launched myself into writing my first few books, solving every writing difficulty I could see. I have a photograph somewhere of the bed in our spare room which I covered with books. A wiser friend warned me not to publish too much too soon, but I believed that I saw problems, whether in the archives, or in theory, which others had missed, and I determined to tackle them directly. I approached my writing, as I had run, with no capacity for self-restraint.

The union position was beyond me. At first, simply by properly advertising the meetings, I pulled in a fresh group of union members. Attendance was good, some of our larger meetings attracted more people than we had as members in the college. But towards the end of my first year, the college determined to close an entire department, and I lacked the roots to pull off a successful strike. The meetings were large and our ballot came out in favour of working to rule, but against the strikes needed to save the jobs.

My second year was spent fighting managers who had reasons for cuts and were emboldened by their victory. I was representing more and more colleagues in routine casework. The effort of restraining the college managers I found exhausting, and I lacked the skills to turn the situation around.

At the end of the year, the college proposed a single redundancy: the non-extension of my own fixed-term contract. Someone with the deep tenacity of a true long-distance runner would no doubt have fought and might even have won. I was relatively content to negotiate a severance package, within a few weeks I had found myself a new job.

The following spring, by which time we were living in Brent in London, my partner and three work friends entered the Reading half marathon. I was temporarily injured. I waited with the others as they prepared and watched my partner as she ran. I learned, as thousands of others have, how tiring it is trying to spot one person in a crowd of runners. You look and you see faces and each one seems the same.

The next year I ran the same event, together with the same group of friends. It was strange to find myself in a crowd of runners, unable to pace myself but having to run at the same speed as a large group. If I wanted to go more slowly, I would find another runner's knee in my back. If I wanted to go run faster, there was no gap through which I could squeeze.

As the crowd thinned I paced myself as best I could. The first six miles I ran in an hour. The seven miles back, I let myself stretch, finishing the half marathon in one hour 50 minutes. It was a mediocre, fun runner's time and I was delighted with it.

In the six months leading up to the race, I had come closer than ever before to completing a proper winter's training. I began by running no more than a couple of times per week, typically for two or three miles a time. Slowly, I built my distance up, until I was running up to five times a week, with a Sunday run of up to 20 miles, and a total distance of about 40 miles each week.

At my peak, ten years before, I had run much faster and I had been capable of running further than I could now bear. I kept fit on the track, then, not on the road. The hardest thing was finding the time to build up my distance. A running textbook might tell you that a runner should always run 60 miles per week. But at my typical jogging pace, that would be ten hours per week, on top of which I would need a further five or ten hours' warm-up and warm-down time. I was working, I did not have the time to run that many miles.

I had also begun to feel a fresh set of pains in my left knee.

My mother had clipped for me an advertisement from her newspaper for a joggers' aid which promised to minimise the risk of injuries by placing runners in special boots above a giant rubber spring. I could recall the lightness in my legs when I had run in my teens, the bounce I made on the track at my peak. I responded enthusiastically to her suggestion and a week later was opening a shiny black pair of kangaroo boots.

The first surprise was quite how high the boots took me off the ground. I ran an entire foot taller, even more indeed at the peak of my bounce. At least at the start, it was a real battle not to fall over mid-way through my stride. I was a stumbling, happy giant, friends laughed to watch me run.

The boots undoubtedly protected my tendons, for which I was grateful. Unfortunately, they also placed new pressures on the sides of my feet: they were, after all, heavy. I noticed that they accentuated old problems I had had with the cartilage on the sides of my knee. A runner's aid, intended to protect me against further injuries, seemed to be making things worse.

I ran often along the canals that ring the boundary of central

London. I would jog East from Kensal Green, through Little Venice, to Regent's Park. I built up my stamina until I could run two full laps of Regent's Park before returning home. Sometimes I would run West along the canal towards Ealing. The air was fresher near water. There were herons at the top of the buildings as I ran past. I could run some of the way on grass, which was more forgiving but less reliable than concrete. When it rained, my shoes would slip in the mud. I feared tripping and spraining my ankle.

I shared the canal path with cyclists, as they approached I held my body to the inside as their bells rang past. I ran past locks and sluices, I balanced on the narrow beams. Cars passed loud above me on the bridges, I ducked my head down.

My real ambition was not the half marathon, delighted as I would be when I had finished that race. Without any considered plan save the desire to be able to say I had completed the distance, I had entered to run the full London marathon.

After Reading, my knee was once again too sore for me to run. The problem was that there were just six weeks to the marathon, and I doubted I would recover in time. I found a physiotherapist, who set to work on my knee, using the same ultrasound devices with which I was familiar from my achilles injuries years before.

To keep my heart and lungs fit while the treatment took effect, the physio suggested that I practise on one of his exercise bikes. This I did, in one hour slots, with the bike at maximum resistance. The look the physio gave me suggested that he found my injury hard to credit, if I could keep myself going at that rate, what really was wrong? After three or four lots of ultrasound, the injury was cured. Yet my knee and my legs remained weak, and I was nervous of trying to get back into running too fast. Even simple training before the marathon, I thought, would end in further injury.

As the race neared, I practised stretches, experimenting even for a time with yoga. I swam daily. For my entire six week recovery period, I did not dare run once.

My partner and a good friend Leo took me to the start. I had my running things, a spare woollen sweater and my mobile phone which I later found ruined in an inch of water which had drained into my bag from an unsealed bottle.

Greenwich Park was full of people warming up by running in every direction of the compass, save the route you might have expected us all to follow, East from the park and out. I found my allocated starting point. All our possessions were loaded onto a lorry to be delivered to the race's end. Having bagged up my clothes, I collected a device to record the moment at which I actually crossed the starting line. There were many runners in all sorts of fancy-dress costumes. To get from the assembly point to the start took a further ten-minute run.

My strategy was forced on me by the time I had spent injured. I intended to run the first six miles so slowly that I ought not fall apart later. This was easier than I had anticipated. Caught in the middle of a large crowd, my first two miles passed in a wonderfully slow 25 minutes.

The third mile passed in ten minutes. In Woolwich, I found a house where students had erected a barbecue in their front garden, the rich smell of cooking food floating in front of the crowd. I ran away from the distraction, completing the fourth miles in eight minutes, probably my fastest mile of the whole race.

I passed three Elvises, two red houses for Shelter. Other red houses sped past me. For most of the race I attempted to keep my pace steady at around 10 minutes per mile. To stop my body hurting, I drank water at every stop. Kindly spectators handed out fresh oranges, a short burst of energy, which faded quickly. Processed sugar proved to be the most efficient anaesthetic. I was grateful to the young boy handing out boiled mints. They endured, melting slowly on my tongue.

I had been placed in a group of fellow marathon rookies. Until about the 20-mile point, I seemed to be overtaking the runners immediately in front of me. This did not mean I was fast, the crowds were too thick to push through, and whenever I pushed on I just found myself stuck behind a further slow group ahead.

From four miles in, I passed runners even worse prepared than me. Some were stopping and starting, pushing themselves forwards in 100 metre bursts. I overtook others who had given up altogether on running, and just walked on grimly.

I enjoyed the pavements, which were full of well-meaning onlookers, adults, children of all ages. I despised the roads, they were my enemy. I remember a stretch of cobble-stones, on which my feet could not even land flat. My feet turned to blisters, my knees ached with pain. I loathed Steve Ovett, I swore down vengeance on Eric Liddell and Harold Abrahams. I cursed Phidippides. For much of the race I was wondering how practical it would be to just stop, and exit the race with dignity. I looked hopefully on portable toilets, pubs, but none offered an anonymous exit.

I finished the race in the slow time of 4 hours, 24 minutes. Three months before I had been hoping to run the distance around an hour faster. My brain was always harking back to the runner I had been but was no more. It remains the only marathon I have run, I have never since wanted to run a second.

A year after entering the London marathon, I signed up for a second half marathon in Reading. Through the winter, I kept up a decent routine of about 20 or so miles per week. I had covered more miles a year before, but the end result had been further injury. Mostly, I ran with the Serpentine running club, in large groups of every age and ability, which reminded me of nothing so much as my winters, years before, with Joe.

I travelled down with a school-friend Luke, the two of us talking football as he drove. It rained hard in the second half of the race. We ran most of the distance together until at 10 miles I bored of a pace which I found slow. Charging off into the distance, I completed the race in a time of 1 hour 41 minutes, a nine-minute improvement on my time from the previous year. I would have been even happier for the time had it not been for the (coincidental) presence in the race of Alexis. He had passed me at around six miles, finishing a further ten minutes ahead of me.

Alexis was three years younger than Luke or me.

One of the joys of running with Luke is his refusal to tolerate the limitations of his own body. "I am training for the Olympics in 2012", he once told me, his face dead-pan. "I would never enter a race unless a part of me believed I could win."

One drunken evening, we shared a meal with two other old friends from school, Sadanand, another former middle-distance runner, and Ed, now a tennis coach. Ed told us that he had taken up jogging and was running 40 miles a week, far more than Luke, Sad or me. We pulled out of the main course and sprinted drunkenly along a 100-metre course of our own making. We returned, all coughing, for the main course. The owners of the taverna were less surprised by our sudden departure than by our belated return.

Luke has a long stride. What he lacks as a sprinter he makes up by keeping a steady pace over a much longer distance than I can manage. Within a year of our half marathon together in Reading, he had run his own London marathon, finishing in around three-and-a-half hours, a whole hour faster than I had managed in 2003.

On another occasion, Luke reported back to me on his first

efforts as a triathlete. The event opens with a swim, builds up to a cycle and then concludes with a run. He trained, as I imagine I probably would too, by concentrating on the element in which he could do best: the run. Entering his first triathlon, Luke was astonished to discover the competitiveness of the other athletes. Swimming in more of a curve than a straight line, he was overtaken by the swimmer in last place, who promptly pulled Luke down by his ankle, filling his lungs with water. Luke spluttered his way on, finishing the stage five minutes adrift, in last.

Luke reached dry land, changing into cycling shorts, the other competitors, all better prepared than him, had racing bikes with proper cyclists' shoes. Luke had trainers like bricks, and a friend's pedal bike complete with space for a pannier at the back. The cycle component too he finished last.

Finally reaching the running stage at which he felt most comfortable, Luke completed a 5 kilometre race in a decent time, coming within sight of the runner in second last, who Luke almost (but did not quite) catch.

As for Alexis, he trained for the marathon with a greater sense of purpose than I had managed. Building up his miles through the winter, he found himself running first 30, then 40 and ultimately 60 miles per week. On long Sunday runs he would manage 20 miles regularly without difficulty.

Alexis even raced on the track, building up strength, as we all had fifteen years before, by interval training. Publicly, he committed himself to breaking the three-hour barrier. Privately, I suspect, he thought he was capable of running around two hours forty minutes, faster in other words than he had run at Reading, but off the back of a full winter's training.

The race itself turned out much worse than he had hoped. Lamed by knee pains in the month building up to the marathon, Alexis managed to complete six miles to his original schedule. His body hurting, however, he had to reduce his pace to a jogger's speed. After another six miles or so, worn down by the effort of running in pain, he gave up. By far the fastest runner now out of all three of us, he still has not completed a marathon, save in training.

Among its other events, the Serpentine running club has a regular seven-kilometre "handicap". The idea is the same as the one that I first encountered in my gym classes with Jimmy, all those years ago. The race is supposed to build up to a giant sprint finish, with competitors of every standard capable of winning. I entered the event for the first time in the summer of the year following my marathon entry.

Starting near the back, running in a figure of eight around the Hyde Park lido, I completed the distance in around thirty-and-a-half minutes. It was a time that I would have comfortably bettered right at the start of my running career when I was just fourteen years old. Yet I was delighted with it. Here was a real base; I had been running for two years without serious injury, I longed desperately to keep going.

Around this time, my partner became pregnant for the first time. At one race I overheard a pregnant member of the running club discussing the break she herself would take from running. "But the new buggies are so well designed", a friend answered, "you can take them on a five mile run."

That September, I ran the Serpentine seven-kilometre race in just over 27 minutes, more than three minutes faster than my time the year before. The improvement was so great that I finished second in the competition, probably my best race since I had last run for real, thirteen years previously. I heard other runners muttering to one another that the handicap system made life too easy for runners like me who were only just getting involved in the club.

Shortly afterwards, I finished a 7.2 mile fun run with the club, from Speaker's Corner to Kensington Gardens, Hyde Park Corner, Green Park and St James' Park and back in a perfectly respectable 53 minutes.

I ran on the six-lane track at Willesden stadium. I teamed up with another athlete, roughly ten years my senior. Together we raced a series of 80-second laps. My face was red, my body wet with sweat. I was so happy to be running on a track at all. One of the coaches even took me aside and encouraged me not to overdo it. Had I just been able to continue, who knows, I might have become a shadow of the runner I had previously been.

Around this time, after my first marathon, my then employer agreed to pay for a yoga teacher who visited our workplace on Tuesday and Thursday lunchtimes. A group of twelve of us joined in. I discovered that my most flexible joints are those in my lower back. I was reminded that my upper body is weak, and that my balance is poor. I barely seemed to be able to rotate my left shoulder at all. Comparing myself to others in the group, several of whom were two or three decades older than me, I was disappointed to see just how much less flexibility I had in my legs and in my calves in particular, than they did. These weaknesses acknowledged, I soon learned that yoga suited my running admirably. It was a chance to properly limber up, to stretch deeply. For a pleasant year or two, I ran without suffering tendon injuries.

I signed up to further yoga classes on the weekends and evenings.

Through the winter of the following year, I trained. I did not want to run another marathon, but I looked forward to further half marathons, and I also had plans to resume training on the track.

Back with the Serpies in Hyde Park, I ran another seven-kilometre race. The route took us away from the lido and then back to it. There were long stretches of road and then the sight and sound of water. I remember the thrill of chasing down and overtaking other, slower runners. I remember feeling balanced in my body and light on my feet. I can also remember being overtaken by runners who had started several minutes before me, and the effort I took trying to follow them. For thirty seconds perhaps, or a minute, I kept up, but my body lacked the power to match their pace and I drifted behind. When the race finished, I thought that I had beaten my time of a month earlier. As it happened, I turned out to have run the distance a full minute slower than I had before.

I had been determined to run at full speed. My time had felt fast enough to me mid-race. My running lacked fire, I was relieved to be done.

By now the possibility of my partner's pregnancy was growing into something more definite. She had missed her period. Her body was beginning to feel heavy.

In the New Year, I ran another Serpentine seven-kilometre race. By now, I knew at least some of the other runners, and we chatted before and after the race. I was in my early thirties. Most of the others were younger than me. When I ran, my body itself covered with sweat. I felt broken and old when I finished. My finishing time was twenty-nine minutes, another minute slower again than I had just run.

I travelled home afterwards by bike. I was spending more hours per week in exercise, of one form or another, than I ever had. I had signed up to a gym. Each morning and evening, I had a 40-minute cycle to and from work. I cycled fast through the London traffic, competing with myself from morning to morning by counting the number of buses I overtook. I was twice knocked down by cars during the rush hour, and once I was even caught in a gust of wind so sharp that I went over, head-first, landing on my back. I watched as my bike fell towards my face.

If I was going to keep fit, I knew I needed to do more than just run.

A month later, I was with Luke in Hastings for another half marathon. No-one had warned me that the start and the first three miles were all uphill and the race only slowly flattened out. Unusually for me over any sort of distance, I had a negative split: in other words, I ran slightly faster the longer the race went on. The first five miles I ran in 44 minutes, the next eight miles I ran in 66 minutes. My body felt nimble at the end of the race. My legs were relaxed, it was months if not years since I had last suffered any sort of injury. On the way back to London, Luke shared with me his plans for further triathlons and told me about his success in the marathon.

Joining in with the Serpies for a Saturday fun run, I confided in a fellow runner how much I missed my days as a proper track athlete. Don't worry, she told me, at 35 you'll become eligible for the veterans' races. I've seen it time and again, how people enjoy their running when they race people their own age.

If that was the future, I would welcome it.

In April of that year, I found myself running along the Regent's Canal near Caledonian Road in Islington. My legs felt absolutely content. I had been running for five years. I was fifty metres from the nearest bridge. The day was bright and dry. I felt utterly confident in my body. I saw another runner, a couple of hundred metres ahead and determined to catch up with him. I let my stride lengthen. I let my calves work harder, forcing more energy out of my body as I moved. I was used to running miles at around eight-minute-per-mile pace. My body felt right, the thought occurred to me that I could pick the pace up further. I determined to sprint to the nearest bridge.

I thought that I was in the same condition of utter concentration that I had last been in during that my final 1500-metre race fifteen years before. In my trainers, on the grass, then on the path, I was running the equivalent of a six- or even a five-minute mile. Enjoying the unfamiliar experience of speed, I encouraged myself to dig a little deeper. I was absolutely calm in my body.

I wanted to run faster.

A long suppressed memory passed through my brain. There was a dull pain in my left foot again, around the heel. Instinctively I tried to reduce my pace. The dull pain gave way to something new. Suddenly, I was properly, horribly sore. It was as if some malevolent spirit had pierced my skin with a discarded can. The pain reached from my ankle right up to my lower spine. I turned for home. Walking a little, jogging a little, I tried to keep going. For some reason, I determined not to stop suddenly. I managed 100 metres or so of jogging, as I made my way home. When I had reached the end of the canal, and as I returned to the road, I walked. It was the weekend; the street was empty of pedestrians. My left leg remained in intense pain.

The pain was to remain me with for weeks on end. A further period followed afterwards in which I was no longer sure whether I was still in pain or not.

I had injured my tendon so badly that I would not be capable of running for months. I did not in fact run again for six years.

Boys

On becoming a father, the story of my life was pressed sideways by the stories of those around me. Our first-born son was 18 months old and had gone straight from crawling to running without pausing in between. Our plan one holiday was to hike together around a Lancashire mill, the boy being carried on a backpack. But when the car stopped and our son had been unstrapped, he ran, his legs pounding, his arms waving at each side. He was hopping as much as running; he was charging to escape, with the desire above all to be the master of his own destiny. Within two metres, he had tripped and fallen. He howled, howled and howled.

The reason the fall hurt so badly was that our son had unluckily fallen straight onto his left front tooth. For the next four-and-a-half years the legacy of our son's fall was a grey incisor, not quite dead, but very slowly dying.

Finally, one weekday evening, not long after his sixth birthday, the grey tooth fell out. It was the same size as a piece of boiled sweetcorn. The root had rotted away altogether. Beneath the enamel there was an angry, red void.

It was similar after our youngest son was born. At nursery one of the play workers built a slide. The children clambered onto a low table, no more than 50 centimetres above the ground. From there, a plastic slide would take them back to the ground. Our youngest was standing on top of the table, waiting his turn. He slipped, and was off-balance as his feet hit the ground. Just in that short drop, he turned his ankle. My partner was called, and the poor boy was taken home.

The next morning, he attempted to walk. He could stand, but as he moved his right leg forward his left gave way beneath. He fell, confusion in his eyes. He was taken to the hospital; the scans did not reveal a break.

Afterwards, the boy shuffled forwards on his knees, crawling with his upper body only, or keeping uncharacteristically still. We had to plan his days without the usual weekend expedients, a bicycle ride, a journey by scooter, trips to the park, to the playground or to the leisure centre. Previously, he would chafe against his straps and demand to run. Injured, he sat still in his buggy, far from content.

The doctor viewed the X-rays of the boy's left leg, showing no signs of a fracture. He saw our son, lying in his buggy, playing with a train, his feet dangling beneath him. For days our son's feet had not touched the ground, my partner explained. The boy had taught himself a second time how to crawl. He had learned to walk not on his feet but on his knees. Even the right foot, not supposed to be injured, showed signs of swelling. When we asked our child if his foot hurt, he said yes. He asked for medicine to cure the pain. When we asked if this was why he was not walking, he said yes. My partner wanted to know when he would heal. My own view was that the leg might be broken.

The doctor took our child's train from him, and placed it on a table, two metres away. A look of resentment flicked through our son's eyes. "Will you walk to your train?" The child left his buggy, rose and … walked.

Be careful with your body I want to say to him, the bones you weaken now may remain weak for years to come.

At primary school, many of my eldest son's contemporaries would spend their mornings before class challenging each other to 50-metre sprints, from one end of the playground to the other. The far end was undergoing building works, and you could hear the children crashing into the metal fencing. One boy was the tallest of our son's friends and probably the best runner, and I also followed a second runner, barely half the first boy's height.

The younger boy had a stride out of proportion to the rest of his body. His finger-tips pointed to the sky as he ran.

At the end of year one, it was sports day. The letter from the school told us that our son should bring his gym kit and plimsolls. Our eldest had been entered in two races, an egg-and-spoon competition and a relay race, the latter in a small group of friends.

We spent the weekend preceding the event at a conference, at which a crèche was provided. Walking into the building, the boy tumbled, gashing his knees. Afterwards he could not bend them, ruling him, I assumed, out of the school competition. In the end he did run, happily, his team triumphed.

I doubt our youngest will ever be a runner. He is a strong boy whose favourite task is climbing. At two-and-a-half, the muscles in his chest and arms are well defined. He practices on the bus in the morning, holding himself off the ground by pulling on the plastic bars. He and his brother compete: the eldest holding on for as long as he can. Generally our eldest wins, but he should do. He has the better balance after all of a six-year-old.

Our youngest is strong for his age. At the playground, there is a climbing frame. He insists on pulling himself four, five metres above the ground. Another allurement is the ten-metre long slide which the children ascend by way of three dozen concrete steps, wholly unprotected by any safety barriers at the side. "When I was born, in the café", our youngest tells me, "I was big and strong."

At his nursery, he tries desperately to be involved in a leaving cohort of the very oldest boys. They tolerate him; my best hope is that he will be accepted by the next micro-generation, who will be the oldest through the next summer, before it is his turn.

I can imagine our eldest running in the years ahead. He has an ability to concentrate on a task. When he was two, we found him staring at the back page of a small Thomas the Tank Engine book. In tiny pictures, barely larger than postage stamps, were the other 40 or so books in the series. Go on, I asked him, what are the trains' names? "Edward", he began, "Henry, Gordon". Without pausing, he continued, "James, Percy, Emily", and so it went on. He learned to read in year one with the same determination, skipping years of reading ages in just a few weeks.

Few people run competitively who have had the choice of other sports at which they also excel. Our eldest avoids cricket and football, the younger boy enjoys them, joining in with others as they play.

A decent runner will have a strong heart and lungs, of course, strong legs, and an unfussy running style. They will be able to race, repeatedly, without suffering injury. These qualities are necessary rather than sufficient. Above all, every decent runner I have ever met has the same focus, the same ability to drop everything for a single goal.

Now

Until this spring, I had not run for six years. As of this month, I find myself running again. Now, I run most weekdays before leaving for work. I have just enough time to warm up, run, and bathe on my return. I do not altogether understand why I have resumed. The gap I find easier to explain: I stopped running on the birth of my first son. I had not been running much before he was born. I had suffered a series of injuries and was out of sympathy with the sport.

After my son's birth I lacked the energy to run. There was a new life. My son had needs, to be loved, to be hugged, to be fed. My partner had needs too, above all to sleep. The time when I might have been running I was with my son. And then the whole experience began anew: my partner was pregnant again, our second boy was born. There were two new lives around mine, each more exciting than my own.

This April, I found myself running again. I have allowed myself occasional rest days since and sometimes I have been injured. But, despite setbacks, I keep going.

One day, I feel pains all along the left side of my knee. I respond by starting my pre-run warm up before going to sleep the night before. I then warm up for a second time before beginning my run in the morning. The longer I spend on warming up, the deeper I stretch. Yet even on good days, I find that my left ankle is stiff, and the tendons around it swollen. I wonder if I will again be able to touch my toes.

To vary my run, I keep the distant constant, but intersperse - in the midst of a long run at a comfortable speed - short bursts of fast running, almost sprints, followed by walking or jogging to recover. After three days of running at varied pace, I extend the faster mini-sprints up to a cautious 50 metres. Maybe in another month I will stretch the sprint to 100 metres. I have to remind myself repeatedly to run at the pace my legs will allow, not the speed that my brain recalls.

Another morning, my brief jog leaves my calves feeling so stiff and sore that for the following two days I do not dare run.

My boys ask to be taken to a sports centre; they intend to spend their time chasing each other up and down slides, or into pillars coated in layers of primary-coloured foam. They break at half hour intervals, demanding water in the first, and one of the centre's iced fruit drinks at the second. My eldest fills himself with liquids, making up for the sweat he has worked off.

Arriving at the building early, I see a runners' noticeboard, full of posters advertising 5k and 10k races, half marathons and marathons. Even if I were to maintain and develop my present routine and even if I could build up my speed or my distance, I am far away from wanting to race alongside other runners.

I have run before and I have injured myself. I have quit running so many times. Again and again, I have pushed myself too hard, mis-reading my body. This time, I have no grander ambition than to get a year's running into my legs. I want to start at an average intensity and maintain it. I just want to get my body fit enough so that I could start to think about challenging myself again.

When I ran my one marathon, I learned a little about carbo-loading, the idea that before a big race an athlete should over-fill with pasta, rice or potatoes, and give up fats and protein. The bulk of the carbohydrate is burned up quickly when your body works at near maximum energy. I have tried carbo-loading and have seen it work. A runner can convince their body that it has a surfeit of energy.

When I ran at school, I had the same diet as all my contemporaries, sporting or otherwise, save only that I was an early vegetarian. I even spoke with the unfortunate person whose job it was to plan our meals with a budget of little more than £2 per student per day. She did not buy many fresh vegetables.

Today, my diet is something I barely control. I am at work most nights until late, and even if I packed myself a lunch, my evening meals would still be chosen from various categories of shop-cooked meal. On weekends, I try to cook for the boys but they compete however to narrow their diets, disdaining vegetables, potatoes. I have to limit my diet to foods they might eat.

When I ran, my weight was always just a little over 10 stone. Within five years of stopping, my weight had settled at thirteen stone, where it then remained for most of the next two decades. Eighteen months ago, on starting my present job, my weight began to fall, and in the first six months I lost an entire stone. I am a barrister now, the hours are long. I work at a high intensity. I am often instructed at short notice and work late. There is no time to think about food. Since starting my weight has stabilised at twelve stone.

For most of the past eighteen months, my weight has been very steady: through Christmas mornings too cold to walk to work, and through bright summer days, when I have walked and I have been eating less.

On my resumption of running, and as it has started to become a habit again, my weight has begun to mount upwards. I watch the scales warily. My metabolism is working faster, I am sure, and I drink more water. Maybe I am adding muscle, I certainly hope that my legs are regaining muscle definition. Perhaps, I am also eating more.

A reason my weight does not fall is that although I am running more regularly, I keep myself to short distances and low speeds. Even if I keep on running, it will be months before I dare try track running or proper miles.

Any track work, even the most gentle, would cause me to pick up an injury within days. I need to teach myself again how to run. Distance running ought to be simpler, it is just a matter of building up the miles at the rate of 10 percent or so a week. Yet I recall the club I joined in my early thirties, and the advice a fellow team member gave me, "Don't run marathons. The people who give the sport up are the ones who try to run too far for their bodies." Guides to running marathons encourage a routine of 60 miles per week. Runners need to accustom their body to long distances if they want to sustain any pace for a marathon. But running on this scale wears out your joints and tendons. It is more than most runners can take.

I remain a middle-distance runner. I have never enjoyed running any real distance.

There is a picture in my bedroom, it was taken seven years ago. I was photographed on the last hundred metres of a half-marathon. It had been raining, and behind me you can see a whole stadium of people all sensibly wrapped in plastic, water-proof clothes. I wore a thick woollen sweater, which was now cold and heavy, saturated with rain and sweat. The time was not so fast that I would have been proud of it at my peak, nor so slow that I could match it now. I am running above a white sheet, draped over an old synthetic track. I was nearing the finish, and there is joy as well as relief in my face. You can see me trying to pick my knees up to race for the line

Scanning my photograph, I note the fatigue in my body and my poor technique. My head is to one side, my chin is too high, and my standing leg seems ominously straight. My left hand is going sideways almost as far as it goes backwards. I can see that I was over-rotating my hips.

It was bad enough then: I would refuse to be photographed running now.

When I run now, my route takes me out of my house, along 150 metres of concrete to a road, then more concrete and a park. I run past a playground, past the clock tower at which some of London's first trade unionists gathered to demonstrate their solidarity with the exiled Tolpuddle martyrs of the 1830s, up the slightest of hills, along grass, over tracks made of earth mixed with stone.

One day I find a football, discarded at the base of the hill. I try to dribble it up the hill but find that kicking it so disturbs my rhythm that I give up and side-foot the ball away. I return to the same park with my sons. I come back to the park with my partner on those precious romantic evenings we spend alone. The spring has been dry, but the ground gives a little beneath our feet.

Other runners come equipped with devices on their arm to measure their pace, the distance they have run. They wear headphones to distract themselves from their bodies, they look down and do not smile as we pass. Unlike them, I acknowledge my lack of pace, the weakness of my legs.

When I warm up, I start by rolling my neck clockwise and then anti-clockwise in circles. I then do the same with my shoulders, at first with my arm outstretched and then, faster, with my arm bent at the elbow. I rotate my hips, first with my knees held straight, and then with knees bent. I hold my body straight, dropping my head and chest first to one side and then another. To loosen my legs, I kick up and out from my heels. I rotate my ankle in circles. I hold my legs apart and drop my hand towards my toes. I stand tall pointing my toes high.

From an assistant in a runners' shop I once learned to hook one leg in front of another, bend down at the waist, and lift my arms above my head. This unnatural movement is supposed to protect the cartilage on the outside of my knee.

I have also picked up a series of stretches based, albeit very loosely, on a tai chi class I once took, more than ten years ago.

They do my body little good, I suspect, but at least in controlling my breathing I let my chest relax.

Five weeks or so back into running, some of the training is beginning to take its effect, muscle development is returning to my legs. When I practise my stretches, I find that my body can relax more deeply than it could. The progress is slow, however, and there are many setbacks. My week is disrupted; one Monday, I run and my calves are sore. I stop until Thursday, and determine to run, my legs feeling better. By Thursday afternoon I am sore again. Saturday, it is the same again. Before I run, my legs feel just about recovered. Afterwards, I am sore and I wonder how long I will need to rest before I can run again.

The ground is wet underfoot, and as I ascend a gentle hill, running beneath trees covered with dew, the air feels better, cleaner than I have breathed in weeks. I would love to be stretching my legs. I distrust my body and doubt my own capacity for recovery. I do not dare to run freely.

I return to my home to find my eldest laid low by a dry cough. My calves hurt and I worry again that the tendon may be torn.

My left achilles remains sore, the pain arrives just as I start a three-week trial during which I have to leave home at seven every day and only arrive back at around one in the morning. I feel too tired to run, the injury justifies a break which I would have taken anyway. London, in mid-July, turns grey. The murky dark gives me no desire to run. In the same time, I become lazy about my warming up exercises as well. Stretching one morning, I notice that my calves have stiffened once more.

Another evening I walk out with my youngest son just before his bedtime. The sky is cloudy, but it is still light. Holding hands, we enter a small park. Still holding hands we see a small hill, grass laid, presumably, over building debris. We run up the hill, pause at the top, and run straight down. My boy, losing his balance, tugs on my hand to remain standing. We see a second hill and run down it again.

Story time passes quickly, at its end, my son gives me a night-time hug and kiss. Before eight in the evening, my brain cramped, I join him in sleep.

After the three-week gap, I start running again. I begin with a short run of just around a kilometre or so. To my relief, my left calf feels only a little weaker afterwards. The roads are empty of people, a single desultory squirrel crosses my path. The air is cold, I breathe deeply, my lungs tighten as I near the end of my run. I return to find two night-time migrants freshly resting under our covers, the eldest boy genuinely knocked out, my youngest boy "playing sleep". He wriggles from his waist, sending his legs flicking and kicking at unpredictable intervals onto my partner's stomach. "My lum chop, smarties", he sings.

Above and between the black railings of the park, at intervals, are odd black pointed lumps of sculpted iron. Looking at them briefly from a distance, they remind me of nothing so much as a series of policemen's helmets. Looking at them a second time with more care, I am relieved to see that there is nothing sinister about them.

The sky is grey, the winds blow in from the North. A month wasted, I am barely nearer to fitness than I had been when I started running again.

In a dream I meet Paul with whom I used to run. He still has the physique of a runner. He has changed less in 20 years than I have in real life. Join me, he says, and the two of us set off for a run. Waking, I take the dream literally, and restart my morning runs. I jog a short distance, finding that all I can manage is a hobbling, halting pace. I have to work my arms hard to maintain any momentum. My left achilles seems stiff, as ever, and I have memories of when my leg was broken and it could not support properly my weight.

In the last few weeks, my eldest has developed a sudden taste for swimming. Having hated the feel of goggles tight on his head, the boy suddenly decides they are a necessary evil. His favourite game is now to fish locker keys from the bottom of the pool. Once, he manages to swim an entire length of the pool on his back.

Returning to our home, I am delighted that my legs feel no more than usual pain. I intend to sustain my running through the rest of the week.

Autumn overtakes our pale summer, leaves turn yellow from their tips downwards. I feel just about recovered from my summer of achilles injuries, and build up running in the park once more. Within a week, I find it possible to build up from a single lap of the park to two. The days grow shorter. Returning from work one evening, I am half shocked to see that it is already dark. We replace our light summer blanket with a winter duvet. In the mornings, it is harder to wake. My left achilles remains stiff, but at least it is no longer sore. I am not stopped from running.

It has been said that Milton produced *Paradise Lost* for the same reason a silk worm produces silk. It was an activity of his nature. A runner, it has been said, does not know how or why he runs. He only knows that he must run, and in so doing he expresses himself as he can in no other way. But if you admit this is true, where does it leave the injured athlete, the non-running runner?

I find my bike in my shed, and with Alexis's help, get it ready again.

Charlie once told me that the worst thing for injured runners is not the pain of the injury itself, nor even the frustration of being deprived of the chance to race. The worst part is the uncertainty, for a runner never knows how long the injury will last. When I was at my peak, I suffered injuries which cost me just a week of running, injuries which lost me a month, and injuries which ended my real running career. All you feel is a pain sharp enough to make you stop. You have no idea of its severity. To add to the frustration, the more you train and the faster you run, the greater your risk of injury is.

An injured runner is a chained beast, an advocate mute.

I am distracted from my frustration by my eldest boy's improvement as a swimmer. He has swum daily for a fortnight with his grandfather. Returning to London, he resumes lessons, and we discuss whether he should move up a class. He has swum with my partner and with me. For a period of three weeks, the boy swims six lengths of an improvised mixture of front and back stroke every day.

I take a week off work at the start of September, resting at home with the boys. Collecting our eldest each day after school, he asks to be taken swimming. Much of our time is spent diving for trinkets, toys or our locker keys left on the bottom of the swimming pool. On the first day, as the boy has been doing for a while, he swims six lengths of the adult pool employing his own personalised stroke. The laps begin in a decent approximation of a proper swimmer's start. His arms are in front, his body ripples through the water. He does not breathe.

In the next phase, the boy swims for about a third of the pool, employing a mixture of breast stroke arms and front crawl legs. He does not know how or when to breathe, so his legs drop slowly down until he is treading water. Several deep breaths later, he sets off again. He manages a short distance before having to pause once more.

Around a third of the pool covered, our son finally tires. He swims the remainder of the length on his back. Then, after a further break, he starts to swim again.

I have a plan of sorts to tempt the boy away from an entire week of chlorine. One of his favourite parks offers an after-school calendar of daily sports: football, basketball, tag rugby, athletics, badminton, tennis, trampolining, dodge ball and more. Children show up and join in whichever activity they like. Collecting him from school, enticing him with the prospect of his favourite snacks, I suggest that we break from our usual routine and try one of these instead. He refuses.

The mixture of sports having been rejected, I try to think of an alternative plan to break his routine. I suggest that he might like to swim further than he has before. I propose, and he agrees, that he should aim for a fresh target, eight lengths.

It proves a considerable effort. After six, the boy begins to tire. The seventh lap is swum almost entirely on his back. I walk beside him, telling him how well he is doing and encourage him to try again. There is a long pause between the seventh and eight laps. Then, fatigue overcome, he manages to complete the eighth length. Afterwards, he delights: "I've got my record"', he says, "my world record!"

After two days of his idiosyncratic swimming, I invite the boy to swim differently. We practise breathing, head in the water, head lifted sideways and out. I bribe him with the promise of sweets from a machine. The boy agrees to swim an entire length, and then a second on his side. He takes a float (these, usually, are refused), and swims a sort of crawl, patting the float in front of him in the water rather than holding on.

Seeing my moment, I invite him to swim a length of the child's pool in his best impression of front crawl. This, the boy manages easily. At times, he lifts his head upwards rather than sideways to breathe. Occasionally, he forgets to start his crawl arms properly behind his head. More than once, his arms make something more like breast stroke. But he does not merely cover the distance, he swims.

Then, we try the same in the adult pool. Twice, he manages to swim a full 25 metres, swimming his first ever whole lengths solely on his front. Afterwards, we hug, I am as proud of him for his triumph as I ever was for anything I did myself.

When I run, I feel my legs unstiffen and stretch. I run to luxuriate in the co-ordination of my legs and chest. Like a person meditating, I run to let my head empty of all pressing thoughts. I run for the sudden, temporary exhilaration as I let my knees pick up and my body moves faster, to its goal.

When I was a schoolboy and I ran, I felt that my body was free with the effortlessness of a perpetual-motion machine. Had someone asked me to run from one end of the country to the other, or had I been asked to run an ultra-marathon through a vast, empty desert, neither task would have seemed impossible, I would have only wondered how long it would take me. I knew with absolute certainty that I could run any conceivable distance simply by allowing my pace to slacken and my body to keep going.

Even today, reminded as I am when I run of the weakness in my joints and tendons, the exercise makes my whole body buzz in joy. The effort of work lightens, my skin feels loose. I am taken back to other times and I become young once more.

I run because life is short and there are no moral imperatives save only these: to the weak you owe solidarity, to yourself you owe change. My father in his youth raged against the "bowler hat", by which he meant the prospect of a life predictable from day to day, a life structured always around the same few relationships, a life overwhelmed by the routine of work. He saw that possibility and he rebelled equivocally against it. I share with him that restlessness. A life of movement, he grasped, and I agree with him, is a life fulfilled. A sedentary life is a life voluntarily diminished.

Running has taken me to places that I would not otherwise have seen, it has made the familiar wholly exciting and new. It has taught me a discipline in myself that was all the more powerful because it was embedded in my chest, arms and legs. It has taken me away from the person that I might otherwise have been.

I will be old; I do not doubt that I will be alone. And in that moment, when I look back at my life, I demand the right to reminisce fondly and regret nothing.

I run to see the same city differently. Leaving my house one October morning before breakfast, I find the pavement on which I run deserted. A squirrel, hearing me approach, looks astonished to find her London occupied by any other being. She stares in growing anxiety as I approach. Only when I am almost at her feet does she finally turn and bound away, to the grass, the safety of a tree. In the street, the cars are still. As I approach the park in which I mainly run, I see no people. The grass is damp and the morning cool. I breathe it deep into my lungs. I seem to be able to see further into the distance than the London work-day air usually allows.

The day itself is a work of autumn beauty. I see a tree, its leaves hanging down in showers of copper. Above me, the clouds are low, cut into clumps of cotton. It is a rare privilege to have all this to enjoy, selfishly, alone. My body relaxes into the morning. My stride tentatively lengthens; I work my arms alongside my legs.

I return home to my partner and our boys, I am renewed.

When I run I escape the commodification of life. I dislike the way our social existence is organised, so that merely to live requires you to constantly purchase and consume. Anyone who has had to wait for a few hours in an unfamiliar town will know the frustration of shuffling from one café to another, all the time purchasing little more than a roof over your head for a few minutes at a time.

Sport is a particular culprit. To join a gym, you have to pay a subscription. To watch football, regularly, you should really have a season ticket with your favourite team, or a subscription to satellite television (either will set you back several hundred pounds), or at the barest minimum a much-favoured local and a team playing regularly enough in the right competitions (but few do). Bit by bit, free sport is being removed from television and radio. I am fed up with sports that I watch as a spectator but in which I am not allowed to participate.

To run, all you need is a pair of running shoes (and it is years since I last bought a new pair). The activity itself comes satisfyingly free.

I run because it is my personality, a trait so deep in me that if I leave it unexpressed, I feel a sense of frustration in everything I do. I see in my life the same traits that I exhibited as a middle-distance runner: a capacity different in its way from the short burst of the sprinter or the stamina of the long-distance runner.

My job requires me to assimilate quickly the life stories of my clients, fields of professional expertise, and even sometimes whole fresh disciplines of the law. I soak these up, absorb them, fire everything into the job immediately to hand. The case learned, and the advocacy performed, the task ends. I want nothing more to do with the case ever again. I have joined my profession late, in contrast to those who began in their early 20s, I will leave it without becoming a Judge or a QC. In a case, in my career, I lack the stamina of a long-distance runner, who can perform the same task in infinite repetitions. Unlike them I rejoice when I stop.

With the same joy in creation and the same aversion to the

necessary task of correction, I write.

With just a few other pleasures, running is part of my nature. It is something which I could barely exist without. I run to feel the air cool and my body warm. I run because I want to and because I can. Running has repeatedly surprised me, it has shaken me out of the torpor of daily living. It has strengthened my body and prepared me for days which might otherwise have been stressful or long. At times when I have had to devote every mental effort to a task, running has kept me well.

I have run for the indulgence of physical companionship and I have run to be alone. I have run for the challenge of testing myself, whether against arbitrary goals (such as the time on a stopwatch) or against flesh and blood rivals. I have run selfishly and aggressively at time, I admit, and I have run collectively as part of a team. Running has given me a measure against which to judge myself and others. It has even taught me something of what it means to live well.

I run to live, and when I have run fast my body has been lifted in joy.

There was barely any summer; the days were routinely grey and overcast. Autumn, contrarily, is dry and bright. I extend my morning jog to a more distant park. At its centre, a football pitch is damp with dew, the grass freshly mown. There is a farm in one corner, with cows and sheep and (the undoubted stars) two enormous pigs. I pass a knot of exercise machines, designed to be outside, one in the style of a cross-country skiing device, the others intended to strengthen the exercisers' shoulders or lower legs. I jog past the children's playground. In one corner, there are pressure pads, if you step on them; water shoots out at you and up.

I focus on my body. My stride remains short; I still place too much pressure on my calves. When my foot strikes the ground, it lands somewhere near my arch. For the pace I am running, I should be placing greater weight on my heel. I have been injured off-and-on through the summer and no doubt I will strain my achilles once more. For the moment, however, I run free of complaint.

Step by step, very slowly, I am building up my distance again.

Athletics is barely a team sport. The runner succeeds or fails by his or her own effort, not through the efforts of others. A runner is repeatedly in situations too big to be easily mastered. The difficulties are objective: the barrier of a record, or of a rival, or of a particular qualifying time. If a runner has only limited opportunities to qualify for an event, they cannot succeed by sending a substitute to run the time for them.

A cricketer may seek to preserve their batting average, but their score in any innings is not in their sole control. It is determined rather by their interactions with the opposing players against whom they compete. A slump in the cricketer's fortune can be explained away by hostile weather conditions, the rival team's good fortune, or by any one of a thousand similar petty excuses. I am no worse than I was, a cricketer tells the world; I am the same person in a fresh situation.

A runner, by contrast, races against the clock. If their running goes through a lean patch, for any reason, its evidence is unmistakeable. Their times worsen and there is no-one else who can be blamed.

As you age, your body changes in so many ways and your ambitions subtly alter. I look at my times still, but when I study them, it is not because I retain my old sense than my speed will automatically improve with increased training. Rather, monitoring my times is a means to check my body, to make sure that I am not going too fast and in that way increasing my risk of injury unnecessarily. I take pride at the thought of approximating times I first achieved many years ago. I will never match them, still less beat them, but I do not care.

I have a vision of being able to run in several decades' time. I want to be like Fauja Singh the marathon runner who still goes strong past the age of 100. In my case though, I have determined, I will be back on the track. I plan short distances at high intensity, not roads or hills. My only requirement is that I can find something longer than a mere sprint.

In my imagining, I bounce through the air. My knees are high, my arms force me on. A white beard falls almost to the ground.

I have no desire to run a marathon, even if I keep on improving it will be a whole year before I trust myself to run on the track. There is no-one for me to race, I have let my membership of the Serpentine running club lapse. Even if I could build up my miles, work would not leave me the freedom to run in a group. If I could run further, I know well enough that my body's limits would soon be reached.

My back is sore; when I run I have to take care not to stretch my calves. I have no particular ambition as a runner. If I could run on, I have no larger goal than to feel light in my body, unhindered to move as I like. Let me just run a mile and I can enjoy that feeling. I do not need any distance to feel my body free.

I watch the sunlight through the leaves of the tree outside my house. Soon the leaves will fall and the year will turn. I hear the voices of children. Somewhere, in a playground, a child runs. People are moving through this life, the day begins.

Our youngest boy's nursery school provides a small fleet of wooden bicycles, just wooden frames, with no pedals, wheels or gears. The far end of the playground is set aside as a sort of bicycle track; narrow lanes of flat paving have been cut through a landscape of sand pits, wild flowers and high grass. Our youngest boy races away, using his feet as levers, waggling his hips one way and then the next. At school, at home, or travelling around London's parks and museums at weekends, no adult walking can keep up with him, just to match his speed you have to jog.

The children improvise cycling games, six of them on the bikes, charging from one end of the nursery playground to the other, racing in between one another, dodging the oncoming riders as if they were static, slalom poles. I look, impressed, as the girls and boys just miss each other. Fast as they go, they do not crash.

"Come on my motorbike", one of the children will shout, a signal to the others to raise their legs upwards and tuck them into their stomachs. They hover perfectly balanced, leaving their feet trailing high above the ground.

In the morning, we set off for school. The eldest walks with his school bag in hand. Our youngest refuses to remain in his buggy. He climbs out and runs, his movement taking him from one side of the pavement to the other. "He is running too fast", the eldest complains, "make him wait for me". The youngest boy waits for no-one. "Stop", he says, as we approach a crossing, "there are invisible monsters in the road." The crossing reached, the movement stopped, he lurches off again. He refuses to hold his buggy, refuses to hold his older brother's hand.

Determined to out-think the youngest boy's speed, the older boy holds back, stands, waits. He refuses to come with us; he demands that we remain with him where he stands. We move on, belatedly, he agrees to follow. He tries walking in front of his brother and then stretching out his arms to make the younger boy stop. The youngest, treating this all as a great game, laughs and runs on. Finally, the older boy adopts the same tactic as his brother. He gives me his bag, his coat to hold. He stretches out his arms, his legs.

He runs.

Contemporary culture has eliminated both the concept of the public and the figure of the intellectual. Former public spaces – both physical and cultural – are now either derelict or colonized by advertising. A cretinous anti-intellectualism presides, cheerled by expensively educated hacks in the pay of multinational corporations who reassure their bored readers that there is no need to rouse themselves from their interpassive stupor. The informal censorship internalized and propagated by the cultural workers of late capitalism generates a banal conformity that the propaganda chiefs of Stalinism could only ever have dreamt of imposing. Zer0 Books knows that another kind of discourse – intellectual without being academic, popular without being populist – is not only possible: it is already flourishing, in the regions beyond the striplit malls of so-called mass media and the neurotically bureaucratic halls of the academy. Zer0 is committed to the idea of publishing as a making public of the intellectual. It is convinced that in the unthinking, blandly consensual culture in which we live, critical and engaged theoretical reflection is more important than ever before.